THE SELF AND THE SACRED

THE SELF AND THE SACRED

CONVERSION AND
AUTOBIOGRAPHY IN
EARLY AMERICAN
PROTESTANTISM

RODGER M. PAYNE

The University of Tennessee Press / Knoxville

Library of Congress Cataloging-in-Publication Data

Payne, Rodger M. (Rodger Milton)
The self and the sacred : conversion and autobiography in early
American Protestantism / Rodger M. Payne.
p. cm.
Includes bibliographical references and index.
ISBN 1-57233-015-5 (cloth: alk. paper)
1. Converts—United States—Biography—History and criticism.
2. Christian biography—United States—History and criticism.
3. Autobiography—Religious aspects—Christianity—History—18th
century. 4. Self—History—18th century. 5. Autobiography—Religious
aspects—Christianity—History—19th century. 6. Self—History—19th
century. I. Title.
BV4930.P38 1998
248.2'4'097309033—dc21   97-45426

TO MY PARENTS

CONTENTS

ACKNOWLEDGMENTS

This study began many years ago as a paper in John Corrigan's seminar in American revivalism when I was a graduate student at the University of Virginia. Throughout the many incarnations of the manuscript, Dr. Corrigan has served as its critic and supporter, and the fact that it has finally seen the end of a lengthy process of revision and "re-visioning" is as much a credit to his perseverance as mine. I wish also to thank especially Gerald Fogarty, Valarie Ziegler, and all of my colleagues in the Young Scholars in American Religion Program sponsored by the Center for the Study of Religion and American Culture in Indianapolis. My colleagues at Louisiana State University have been most supportive of this project, and additional research was completed in the summer of 1993 with the support of a faculty research grant from LSU.

Special thanks are due to Briane Turley, who always reminds me that integrity is the foundation of the scholarly life. My wife, Janice, and our daughters, Angela and Jessica, have lived with this project as long as I have and always kept me grounded in the realities of life. Finally, the dedication of this work to my parents is a small expression of thanks for their unconditional emotional and financial support through many years of college and graduate school.

CHAPTER ONE

THE DISCOURSE OF EVANGELICAL CONVERSION

He encouraged me not to fear, and he would tell me how the Lord converted his soul. He informed me that he had struggled with the same kind of fears, and how he labored under the same difficulties and anxieties of mind, and how he found mercy and forgiveness for all his sins.

My attention was arrested. I never had heard the like before. It seemed as if he was telling my own trials.

—*George W. Batchelder, 1843*

This book is a study of the conversion experience in early American Protestantism. The analysis presented here is not intended to confront the definitional issues of what conversion is as much as it is to examine its function within a given community (Anglo-American evangelicalism) at a particular place in time (circa 1740–1850). It is not, however, a chapter in historical theology. Rather, like the Methodist autobiographer George Batchelder, who discerned his own experience in the words of another, I am interested in exploring conversion as a type of "discourse" that was employed by early American evangelicals to speak purposefully of themselves. Whatever its reality as an authentic religious experience, and whatever shape it took in its articulation as a theological or ritual expression, antebellum evangelicals recognized that conversion was also an act of language, a way of saying something meaningful about their lives at a time when traditional conceptions about what it meant to be human were under challenge. My goal, therefore, is not to analyze the experience of conversion itself (presuming such an examination were even possible) but to explore the ways that converts spoke and wrote about their conversions, in an attempt to discern the function that such discourse about conversion played in the formation of the modern consciousness. In short, I will argue that by speaking (or writing) the language of conversion, evangelical autobiographers were able to "baptize" the modern concept of the independent and autonomous self into the larger discourse of Christian orthodoxy. Taking a clue from Batchelder—and from recent critics who argue that linguistic expression actually creates rather than merely represents experience—I want to examine the way that the texts *of* conversion (as opposed to texts *about* conversion) served to constitute self, experience, and community for early American evangelicals.

The years 1740 to 1850 were the formative age for American evangelicalism. By the middle of the nineteenth century, evangelical Protestants predominated—ecclesiastically, politically, and culturally—in virtually all areas of the country; and while the Civil War managed finally to split the evangelical denominations along sectional lines, it did little to lessen the hegemony that evangelicalism enjoyed in both North and South. "The story of American Evangelicalism," wrote William G. McLoughlin, "is the story of America itself in the years 1800–1900." While McLoughlin may be guilty of some hyperbole here, his comment does suggest the tremendous cultural power that evangelicalism held in the United States until recent years.[1] Defining exactly what "evangelicalism" is, however, remains a difficult task. Variously characterized by antebellum and contemporary interpreters as a "discipline," "a coalition of submovements," "an ethos," and "a religiocultural phenomenon unique to North America," evangelicalism was and is a theologically and historically complex movement within American Protestantism.[2] Informed not only by the classical Protestant theology of Martin Luther, John Calvin, and the magisterial Reformers, evangelicalism has incorporated emphases drawn from English and Continental Pietism,

Wesleyanism, and Anabaptism as well. In America, the broad stream of evangelicalism coalesced into a coherent movement in the late eighteenth and early nineteenth centuries, embracing such theologically divergent expressions of Protestantism as the Baptists, the Presbyterians, and the Congregationalists. The variety of primitivist Christian restorationist movements that erupted in the early nineteenth century generally participated in the evangelical ethos. Even the staid Anglican Church had its evangelical proponents in figures such as the Virginia parson Devereux Jarratt, the "Grand Itinerant" George Whitefield, and the Wesley brothers of England, who remained within the Established Church even after their American disciples separated from that communion to form the Methodist denomination in 1784. Given this diversity, identifying evangelicalism as a single movement may be using too strong a term; nevertheless, there existed within these denominations a common emphasis, a specific tone of religious and ecclesiastical life that placed a personal experience of Christian salvation at the heart of their respective theologies. As the restorationist leader Barton Stone commented concerning the great camp meeting at Cane Ridge, Kentucky, in 1801 that helped to define American evangelicalism, the Presbyterian, Methodist, and Baptist ministers there "all preached the same things" and were "of one mind and one soul, and the salvation of sinners seemed to be the great object of all."[3]

Whatever its internal divergences, evangelicalism in antebellum America was part of a larger religious phenomenon that had begun to appear in Western culture in the seventeenth century as traditional corporate and nationalistic forms of religion were in disarray and decline. New devotional forms appeared not only in Protestantism but also in Catholicism, Russian Orthodoxy, and even in Judaism that were characterized by their attention to affective piety as the key to effective religion. In Protestantism, this "religion of the heart" took various shapes—Puritanism in England, the Lutheran Pietism of Philipp Spener in Germany, and the Reformed Pietism of the Netherlands—before bequeathing its heritage to the evangelical groups that began to arise in the mid-eighteenth century in Europe and America. The "great object of all" these movements, to adopt Stone's phrase, was to foster this affective piety by demanding that individuals seek to obtain a personal experience of divine forgiveness and salvation. The redemption of the individual became "more than a forensic act on the part of God," according to one interpreter. "It must enter into human experience . . . in the divinely wrought miracle of conversion."[4]

For American evangelicals, nothing was more important than this experience of conversion because it marked such a decisive transformation in the life of the individual. "The Scripture representations of conversion," wrote Jonathan Edwards in 1746,

> do strongly imply and signify a change of nature: such as being born again; becoming new creatures; rising from the dead; being renewed in the spirit of the mind; dying to sin, and living to righteousness; putting off the old man, and putting on the new man; a being ingrafted into new stock; a having a divine seed implanted in the heart; a being made partakers of the divine nature, etc. . . . They that are truly converted are new men, new creatures; new, not only within, but without; they are sanctified throughout, in spirit, soul and body; old things are passed away, all things are become new.[5]

Theologically conceived, conversion thus created an ontological gulf between the convert and the unconverted, designating nothing less than the absolute appropriation of the Christian promise of redemptive salvation that was a normative and necessarily prior condition of the Christian life. "Men are first redeemed, bought, created, regenerated," asserted Edwards, "and by that means become members of the Christian Church; and this is the ground of their membership."[6] Even for many of the Calvinistic denominations that clung to the notion of divine predestination, an experience of conversion remained the absolute imperative that was demanded prior to joining the earthly communities of the elect.

Engendering and promoting individual conversions was at the heart of the great revivals and awakenings that shook Anglo-American culture in the eighteenth and nineteenth centuries. As the critical center of evangelical belief and practice, the experience of conversion was ritualized and theologized by evangelicals and was the subject of countless sermons, pamphlets, and theological tomes. The contemporary heirs of antebellum evangelicalism have continued to probe the theological meaning of conversion, to examine its evidences, and to hold it forth as an imperative for salvation. The rise of the social sciences in the late nineteenth century brought to bear other analytical perspectives beyond those bounded by such confessional interests, and so in the past hundred years conversion has enjoyed the attention of psychologists, anthropologists, sociologists, historians, and phenomenologists, among others.[7] Offering yet another study of conversion, therefore, requires some justification and qualification.

In examining evangelical conversionism as a type of discourse, I am principally concerned with the way in which conversion language was actually used by evangelical spiritual autobiographers to produce meaning and purpose in their lives. My own understanding of discourse has been informed and enriched by the work of Michel Foucault, particularly his book *The Archaeology of Knowledge,* which attempts to define what Foucault meant by his use of the term. In general, Foucault argues that discourse is nothing more than "a group of verbal performances," but not just any use of words or "signs" constitutes a discourse. Discourse is always a system of linguistic relationships that exists between the "object" of the discourse, the "enunciative modalities" that help establish the conceptual definitions of the object, and the "strategies" or "theories" that provide the ways in which the components of the discourse are brought together into a coherent and meaningful whole. These elements are not formed in temporal or linear relationship to one another, but rather stand within a matrix of mutual reciprocation. Those who are recognized as having the authority to give conceptual definition to the discursive object, for example, receive this authority by speaking on the object, as long as their speech conforms to the larger discursive strategy. As a linguistic activity involving signs, words, and texts that have been shaped according to specific configurations and accorded particular interpretations, discourse thus connotes a way of speaking (or writing) meaningfully—of offering an explanatory model of reality (or at least the way in which reality is perceived) that has gained the widespread approbation and acceptance of a culture, society, or community.[8]

As an explanatory model, discourse can appear within any given cultural setting, but Foucault noted that new discursive formations may arise quite suddenly and almost immediately attain the status of "truth" as they become the basis for analyzing and explaining the human condition. The individual elements of any discourse may have been present for years, even centuries, within the culture but may not have functioned as discourse until the formation of a specific historical context that sanctions the combination of these elements into a meaningful form with paradigmatic value.

When these elements are thus combined and receive the approval of appropriate cultural authorities, a discourse is produced and legitimated and assumes a certain position of power within society that is independent of any individual or social institution.[9] Thus, the process of discursive development involves both a conscious and an unconscious effort that produces a complex and interdependent relationship between the object of the discourse, its conceptual formation, and the authorities that articulate both the object and the discourse.

Foucault's model of discourse has significant implications for the analysis of religion and religious forms. As a primary means of producing and assigning meaning to human existence, religion might be regarded as a type of meta-discourse, and many religious forms—texts, rituals, theologies—certainly perform functions similar to those identified by Foucault as expressive of discursive formations. In Clifford Geertz's famous definition, religions provide both "models of" and "models for" human thoughts and actions in that "they give meaning, that is, objective conceptual form, to social and psychological reality both by shaping themselves to it and by shaping it to themselves."[10] In corresponding fashion, discourse—defined in its simplest form as a way of speaking meaningfully about something—offers both models of reality (that is, how the individual or society is meaningfully conceived) and models for reality (by incorporating new or otherwise problematic ideas and/or events into the existing conceptual forms). This latter function is particularly important when individuals or societies are faced with ideas or events that are potentially disruptive to social order or individual well-being. The religious response to the "suspicion" that things are not orderly, that chaos might plunge all into an abyss of meaninglessness, according to Geertz, is "the formulation, by means of symbols, of an image of such a genuine order of the world which will account for, and even celebrate, the perceived ambiguities, and paradoxes in human experience."[11] Like the sudden eruption of new discursive forms, religions, faced with the need to respond to new and possibly dangerous phenomena, may reconfigure existing elements in the culture into new paradigmatic forms that can take the form of either symbolic activities (ritual) or linguistic metaphors that appear in myths, written texts, and/or dogma.

For Protestants in the eighteenth century and beyond who were faced with significant and often disorienting cultural changes, the discourse of conversion became an important means of speaking to the challenges that they confronted. To adopt Foucault's terminology, conversion emerged as a discursive object in Protestantism as early as the seventeenth century with the rise of various pietistic traditions that emphasized personal and affective experience over sacramental activity as the key to the Christian life. The decline of the sacramental system marked the demise of the corporate structure of Christianity that had for so long dominated Western religious life, and it paralleled the reconstitution of virtually all social institutions and ways of knowing that had characterized medieval life. Between the sixteenth and nineteenth centuries, changes in the theoretical and practical structures of economic, scientific, technological, and political life transformed Western culture, creating a correlative sense of confusion and disorder. Faced with these numerous transformations that delineated the rise of "modernity," many Protestants in Europe and America reconceived traditional religious and ecclesiastical forms as a means of interpreting and making sense of the new cultural phenomena they were forced to confront. For many of these Protestants, conversion became the principal metaphor through which they could incorporate these changes into their worldviews.

Perhaps the most troublesome of these modern phenomenon to traditional Christian forms was the rise of the concept of the "self" as the independent and autonomous seat of human sensation, intellect, and consciousness. The early modern era invested the individual with ultimate, even "inalienable," authority, and expected her to negotiate a vast array of choices made suddenly complex by intellectual, political, and religious revolutions. Increased theoretical and actual opportunities for making choices—what career to follow, whether or not to immigrate, what form of government to institute—meant that Protestants had to rethink their traditional evaluation of human capabilities and moral responsibility. New theological constructions that challenged the rigidity of Calvinism appeared, many still claiming the sobriquet of Calvinist even while exchanging such Calvinist essentials as predestination with "free moral agency."[12] Classical Protestant doctrines such as salvation by faith alone continued to be espoused by the early modern heirs of Calvin, but the emphasis and meaning of this concept had begun to change by the mid-eighteenth century when even grace itself had become a matter of choice to be accepted or rejected by human beings.

The evidence of this change was rhetorical. Adopting a traditional Christian language of sin, grace, and salvation, evangelicals reformed and refined these concepts into a unique discursive form that sanctified personal choice and responsibility. Although the vocabulary was conventional, the conceptual parameters had changed, and in speaking about conversion, evangelicals engendered a new discourse that was specifically directed toward the cultural situation of Anglo-American Protestantism in the late eighteenth and early nineteenth centuries. While continuing to recognize and affirm the traditional Protestant values of personal humility and human inability, evangelicals were able to embrace and sacralize the concept of the autonomous self.

The self was a creation of the early modern West; it was the distinct invention of a new consciousness that was, most fundamentally, narrative in its form and essence.[13] It was, in other words, a creation of modernist discourse. To name something is to ascribe it meaning, and discourse both names and assigns meaning to the unknown by use of the known—not so much representing reality as much as interpreting its disruptions and discontinuities by the use of displaced or even contradictory words and phrases. By so doing, discourse actually "*constitutes* the objects which it pretends only to describe realistically and to analyze objectively ... with full credit to the possibility that things might be expressed otherwise."[14] Presented with some previously unknown phenomenon, some new and discordant event or circumstance, discourse, like religion, provides a way of speaking to—of saying something meaningful about—that which has possessed no prior cultural reality.

According to the analysis of Foucault, there is no inevitability in the shape that discursive formations may take, leading him to speak instead of "ruptures" that create, rather suddenly, new discursive formations from preexisting concepts. Certainly conversion was not an entirely new concept within Christianity; there were both biblical and historical precedents encouraging individuals to "turn away" from sin and to "turn toward" a life of righteousness.[15] But Protestant evangelicalism brought new inflections to this traditional language of sin, grace, and reconciliation with God that borrowed from—but likewise brought new limitations and specifications to—these antecedent concepts. In responding to the new cultural situation of the early modern period, evangelicals came to view the biblical call for conversion in an original and highly experiential way that was significantly different from the conceptual formations that had preceded them. By using the language of conversion, evangelicals meant to "say" something specific and meaningful about themselves and what they perceived to be the discursively constructed reality in which they lived, moved, and had their being.

This reconceptualization of conversion took place at various "sites" (to use the Foucaultian term), where it was articulated by the appropriate discursive authorities. Ministers certainly constituted such discursive authorities, because they spoke from the traditional Protestant sites of the pulpit, sermon, or theological tract. But evangelicals, as participants in a larger cultural reevaluation of self and subjectivism, granted all converts the power to speak about conversion. To claim conversion was to claim the authority to speak of conversion, and even the minister was admonished to "attend to himself first, to see that the work of genuine conversion be perfected in his heart," rather than depend upon the inferior authority of his ordination.[16] By investing the experiencing self with the ultimate power to speak about conversion, evangelicals democratized religious authority and valorized as a discursive site a new vernacular literature of conversion narratives and the spiritual autobiographies.

That this new literature formed the most important sites for the discourse of evangelical conversionism seems self-evident, but these texts are not without their difficulties. The conversion narratives and spiritual autobiographies produced by American evangelicals present numerous interpretive problems, not the least of which concerns their use of a very conventional language of conversion that has left contemporary readers and critics frustrated. The "prevailing generalization about early American spiritual autobiography," according to Daniel B. Shea, protests the unoriginal style and presumes the content of such narratives to be "foreknown and predictable." In her study of women's conversion accounts, Virginia Lieson Brereton disparaged the "similarity of 'plot'" in the nineteenth-century evangelical narratives that made them by default always "success stor[ies]," noting the probable inclination of contemporary readers to reject the story they tell "as impossibly burdened with stock religious language."[17] Indeed, only the most devout true believer or the most dogmatic pragmatist could read even a meager assortment of evangelical accounts and not be convinced of an intentionally imitative design that reflects what Edmund Morgan labeled "the morphology of conversion"; that is, a highly structured and stereotypical paradigm of the conversion experience that was intended to exemplify the models of conversion presented through sermons and devotional guides.[18] This paradigmatic presentation of conversion has never been a neutral element in the narratives. If evangelicals themselves simply assumed a nominalist reading of their texts that presumed the priority of experience over expression, more recent critics have adopted a more instrumentalist reading where function controls both experience and expression. Since the morphology of conversion so intentionally governed the narratives, Brereton asserted, it eclipsed the "strong sense of particular person, of an individual voice" that was so essential to authentic autobiography; and Shea maintained that the "question of grace" could be carefully excised from the accounts without damaging their significance as autobiographies.[19]

The conventional language of the texts of conversion need not be viewed as a liability, however, since regularity and not originality is the goal of any discursive formation. As Gary Ebersole noted in his examination of Indian captivity narratives from roughly the same time period, the nineteenth-century reader of such texts brought a much different expectation to the text than does the contemporary reader. Nineteenth-century readers were not consumers of textual information, but were active participants in constructing the meaning of such texts, and the stereotypes functioned as the means by which "writers were able to make specific claims on their readers."[20] Evangelicals recognized, and endorsed, the paradigmatic and didactic functions of the conventions they utilized in presenting conversion to the reader, and there is no doubt that they intended to manipulate their readers accordingly. But discursive formulas cannot be entirely controlled, and there is sufficient tension within the texts to argue that the language of conversion accomplished much more than the authors intended. In fact, at times, conversion rhetoric actually subverted the intentions of the autobiographers merely to present conversion and demand its replication by the reader. Certainly, evangelical spiritual autobiography and similar narratives of conversion cannot be read as descriptive texts if by this we mean that they give a straightforward account of the author's conversion experience; but neither can they be dismissed as insufficiently autobiographical because they offered only stale reiterations of theological paradigms. To speak (or to write) the language of conversion was to claim the experience of conversion; but, conversely, only the experience of conversion empowered—and compelled—the convert to speak of conversion. Further, the experience of conversion itself became a product of the narrative through which it was given form, structure, and meaning. Within these dialectical tensions between self and experience, and experience and expression, evangelicalism validated the production of the spiritual autobiographies from which the converts spoke with authority. Far from being an inconsequential element of these texts, the language of conversion provided the foundation from which the converts could speak of—and create—themselves. In other words, the discourse of conversion was not a descriptive exercise that pointed to some separately existing reality; it was in itself a part of the linguistic process that constituted both self and experience by naming and ascribing meaning to the disruptions and discontinuities that faced evangelicals in the early modern era.[21]

To speak—or to write—the language of evangelical conversion thus placed the convert within a discursive reality. It also placed him or her within the context of the larger evangelical community that was bound together by speaking, hearing, and interpreting certain words and statements in a particular way. Because evangelicalism recognized—even demanded—that converts should be able to offer a testimony of their experiences, conversion within the evangelical community became a function of language. Only by appropriating the rhetoric and interpretive strategies that had been legitimated and sanctioned by the larger "interpretive community" was the experience of the individual validated.[22] The idealized model of evangelical conversion—what might be termed the "text" of conversion—did not exist as some ethereal authority that was imposed upon individual autobiographers, but was in fact constantly created by the individuals within the evangelical community. Every time an evangelical author described her conversion by using the language of the community she helped to write the larger "text" of evangelical conversion. Each individual conversion was, for evangelicals, a reflection of God's (already determined) redemptive activity, yet each of these separate images was imperfect—not because conversion itself was somehow incomplete or defective, but because it involved that autonomous entity, the self. Despite the very orthodox rhetoric that they employed, evangelical autobiographers repeatedly bemoaned the insufficiency of the language to speak to their individual circumstance, yet they received the sanction of the larger discursive community which verified that they had indeed spoken the "truth" in spite of its ambiguity and irony. To speak the orthodox language of conversion thus brought the evangelical into a shared community of meaning and provided both a model of and a model for a socially constructed reality. By speaking of their conversions—in the oral testimonies and relations, in their written narratives and spiritual autobiographies—converts aligned themselves to these perceived realities.

Evangelical conversionism and the texts of conversion have had tremendous influence on both American culture and literature; yet, despite a presence made remarkable by sheer strength of numbers, evangelical autobiography remains a largely unexplored terrain, its themes and functions all too often presumed rather than critically examined.[23] While the analytical matrix presented here represents a new approach to the reading and interpretation of evangelical Protestant spiritual autobiographies and conversion narratives, it elucidates and illuminates issues that evangelical authors themselves implicitly recognized and struggled to express. In their attempt to master and give valid expression to the self, evangelical autobiographers revealed both a discursive complexity and the modernist dilemma. If the rhetoric of conversion was in many ways contrived and often constricting, it was not for this reason any less authentic when individuals sought to appropriate it to their lives. To recognize the literature of evangelical conversionism as a part of a larger discursive formation is to understand better its function within evangelical life, within a system of linguistic relationships that were ingeniously creative in their response to the cultural challenges of the late eighteenth and early nineteenth centuries. Rather than being simplistic presentations of a routinized paradigm, the conversion narratives and spiritual autobiographies of early American evangelicals were active components in the discourse of selfhood. With the evangelical authors, we must read conversion as the most important part of the narrative, not because we must accept their premise that our own salvation hangs in the balance, but because it was the discursive strategy whereby they gave birth to themselves as both subjects and objects and thus confronted modernity.

EVANGELICAL PIETISM AND THE SUBJECTIVE IMPULSE

In a religious biography the reader expects to find an account of the responsible part acted by the person himself; the treatment he has received from his fellow-men, together with his Christian experience; and how Providence has attended him from year to year. So these works are chiefly designed to proclaim the power of grace; and to show the various gifts and dealings of God to the children of men, in the economy of salvation.

—*Charles Giles, 1844*

When the Methodist minister Charles Giles wrote his spiritual autobiography in 1844, the genre was, as he indicated, already well defined within evangelicalism. The spiritual autobiographer, Giles noted, was certainly not free to write anything he wished; the discourse of evangelical conversionism controlled the way in which the language of conversion was to be produced by the convert and appropriated, in turn, by the reader. This conventional language of conversion posed little problem for nineteenth-century evangelicals, however. Although they knew the linguistic formula well, readers of evangelical spiritual autobiography expected its reiteration; and thus, as Giles indicated, the autobiographer was charged to propagate it correctly. Put another way, the spiritual autobiographers were not in themselves the originators of evangelical discourse; they were functions of it.[1]

The authority of the author to speak about conversion was construed by the discourse of conversion itself. The language of evangelical conversion imposed certain restrictions on the author and limited the range of possible expressions. Discursively, as Giles's readers knew, conversion could take one form, but not another; it could contain some elements, but not others.[2] Despite the prescribed parameters, however, the dynamics between the spiritual autobiographer and the discourse of conversion was not unilateral. A reciprocal relationship recognized the ability of the author to legitimate the discourse according to his or her status as a convert. Such authority—sanctioned within any discourse by tradition, prestige, competence, or by more capricious formulations—was constructed upon two principal foundations: The position of the authority who spoke only from an approved discursive "site," and the perceptual situation of the authority as "subject" in relation to the discursive object.[3]

In early evangelicalism, converts claimed the fundamental authority to speak about conversion; indeed, the experience of conversion compelled the convert to speak. "I think it my duty not to keep silence," wrote the Methodist Freeborn Garrettson in expressing a typical justification for writing a spiritual autobiography, "but to publish to the children of men the great goodness of a benevolent God."[4] Such a self-focused claim of authority presented, however, a contradiction between evangelical autobiography and its theological heritage. Within the Protestant pietist tradition, conversion was understood as a process of self-abnegation, of self-denial; it denoted the utter inability of human effort to contribute to individual salvation. In formulating a story of self, the autobiographer unintentionally but inevitably clashed with these expectations. The theological demand of "humiliation"—the total "emptying" of self that was supposed to mark the attitude of proper conversion—was impossible to achieve when the discourse insisted that converts speak about themselves and thus present themselves as exemplary models of proper Christian faith. Writing an autobiography, even one that attempted to remain within the acceptable parameters of pietistic theology, placed the evangelical author in an untenable position. As one evangelical author expressed in a moment of frustrated candor: "When a man undertakes to write his life, or publish himself to the world, he enters upon a delicate piece of business on many accounts."[5]

This autobiographical problem challenged the author both in regard to the autobiography as a discursive site and to the author's subjective relationship to the discursive object. The question of the author as perceptual subject, as an authority of the discourse of conversion—what I have termed the paradox of the self—will be examined in greater detail in the next chapter. The present chapter concerns the problem of the autobiographical genre as the principal site from which the author presumed to speak the language of conversion.

The sites from which a discourse is "enunciated" can be institutional, documentary, or even statistical. In any case, such sites become the recognized locations "from which [a] discourse derives its legitimate source and point of application."[6] For the evangelical discourse of conversion, the pulpit or theological doctrines were the traditional sites from which the object of conversion could be delimited, defined, and applied. But since conversion was for evangelicals primarily a rhetorical strategy that involved the testimony of the experiencing convert to legitimate the discourse, the "text" of such testimony, whether written or oral, suggests itself as the proper place to begin the investigation of the way in which conversion discourse was enunciated.

The evangelical demand for conversion was a reflection of the cultural moment of the late eighteenth and early nineteenth centuries in Western society. Since evangelicals expected individuals not only to experience conversion but also to be able to give an account of this experience, they participated in the growing concern of an age that not only produced a new awareness of the possibility of subjective self-reflection but also coined a new term—*autobiography*—in order to name it and give it objective substance. Although the activity of autobiography was not in itself new, its appropriation and affirmation by all levels of society was, and so this neologism, noted Jerome Hamilton Buckley, "arose to satisfy a rapidly growing need." The sudden emergence of autobiography as a distinct and newly denominated form of both elite and popular literature near the turn of the nineteenth century was an indication, Buckley argued, "of the rise of self-consciousness throughout society and of a new reverence for the subjective impulse in literature."[7] The objectification of autobiography—best demonstrated in its naming—may be taken as a significant symbol for a culture that was beginning to place substantial emphasis on the validity of personal experience as a key to unlocking the human situation. As one noted nineteenth-century philosopher asserted, "Autobiography is the highest and most instructive form in which the understanding of life confronts us."[8]

Protestant pietism both shaped and shared in this subjective impulse. From the first halting attempts of the Puritans to give expression to their conversion experiences in their spiritual diaries and "oral relations," to the structured pattern of spiritual autobiography that Charles Giles confidently described in his own work, conversion narratives form perhaps the oldest example of the "subjective impulse" in American literature. If this subjective impulse might be read, as some critics have suggested, as implying the modernist conception of the individual as a being always changing, always in the process of transformation, then "conversion" in the broadest sense of the term becomes the essential foundation for—and an appropriate analogue of—autobiographical activity. "[O]ne would hardly have sufficient motive to write an autobiography," Jean Starobinski has argued, "had not some radical change occurred in his life—conversion, entry into a new life, the operation of Grace." Otherwise, the autobiographer could "depict himself once and for all," and the function of the author would be reduced to commentator on "external (historical) events."[9] Only the transforming self constitutes both the subject and the object of proper autobiographical activity.

Autobiography and evangelicalism both appeared at virtually the same time in Western culture.[10] Forms of "self-life-writing" existed long before 1800, of course, but they generally lacked the subjective impulse that defines the genre in contemporary understanding. Intentionally autobiographical writings were rare in the ancient world because the patent "offensiveness" of presenting one's own life as exemplary in some way, and examples of self-focused writings usually resorted to various artifices to disguise, or at least to lessen by elaborate justifications and apologies, such temerity. More common during the Greco-Roman period were ostensibly "biographical" writings that held up an individual other than the author as an *exemplum vita;* but, even here, contemporary conceptions concerning biography cannot be easily applied to ancient forms. The desire to present through a written text the example of a single life was not done under the constraints of achieving historical authenticity, but rather with the express design of personifying some ideal or ethos and encouraging emulation and imitation on the part of the reader. Persuasion and evocation, rather than an anachronistic devotion to historical accuracy and objective description, marked the intent of Hellenistic life-writing. The historicity of the proper subject was incidental to the timeless significance that might be discovered and portrayed by the biographer.[11] In the process of transforming an exemplary life into text, the historical character of the individual was wholly subsumed and the subject was reduced to little more than an idealized type.

Early Christians, not surprisingly, shared in this Greco-Roman understanding of what constituted appropriate forms of life-writing. In the oldest writings of the New Testament, Paul certainly typified the Greco-Roman apprehension toward autobiographical presentation when he offered apologies for his "boastfulness" and disclaimed any unintentional offense that examples drawn from his personal life might present.[12] The gospels, of course, are dominated by the claims they make for the messianic office of Jesus, thus subordinating historical and even geographical accuracy for theological typology. Even in the post-apostolic age, the few "autobiographical" texts produced by Christians demonstrate distinct affinities to classical forms. The second-century apology for Christianity against Judaism, Justin Martyr's *Dialogue with Trypho,* presents a brief autobiographical fragment of Justin's "conversion" to Christianity; but as numerous scholars have recognized, Justin's peripatetic quest through various schools for philosophical truth before finally accepting Christianity is most likely a literary fabrication that is in keeping with the conventional Hellenistic model of the "conversion to philosophy."[13] Aside from the gospels, the most important "biographical" texts were undoubtedly the martyrologies of which the *Martyrdom of Polycarp* stands as the supreme prototype. Like the Greco-Roman biographers, the author of the *Martyrdom of Polycarp* was controlled by his need to typologize his subject, who becomes not only a type of Christ but also a model of faithful discipleship. By the medieval period, when martyrdom was no longer a viable option in a Christianized Europe, the hagiographies continued the theme of discerning the truths of Christianity as they were refracted through the lives of the saints. History, however, was transitory and "accidental," to adopt the terminology of medieval sacramental theology; only the verities of eternity formed the proper "substance" of the hagiography.[14]

The exception to this rule was Augustine's *Confessions,* "the archetypal spiritual autobiography" within the Western Christian tradition.[15] Despite the towering influence of Augustinian thought on the subsequent development of Western theology, however, *Confessions* was anomalous to its time, and the impact of the introspective attitude cultivated by Augustine was passive rather than direct. As Paul Lehmann observed, although *Confessions* was "widely copied, read, and used in the Middle Ages," it was never "effectively imitated." Rather than the introspective search for God through the search for self cultivated by Augustine, his disciples and interpreters in the middle ages found in *Confessions* a model account of the call to asceticism or to the life of mystic contemplation.[16] Deliberately introspective and retrospective writings on the order of *Confessions* characterized no period of Christian history before the rise of the new affective devotional forms in the early seventeenth century gave supreme religious value to personal experience.[17]

The goals and expectations of ancient and medieval Christian life-writing meant that introspective forms of religious literature could emerge only in the modern era, and the rise of spiritual autobiography owed much to the theological formulations of Protestantism. "The religion of Calvin and Luther," alleges Elizabeth W. Bruss, "turned hagiography into autobiography, since it was no longer miraculous works which were the sign of a saint, but faith—a private and personal experience. The drama of salvation was now enacted in terms of individual psychology; the inner life of one man was merely its principal arena."[18] While this was true in a theological sense—the classical Protestant doctrine of salvation by faith alone certainly reformulated the preferred mode by which redemption was made efficacious for the individual—magisterial forms of Protestantism in fact contributed little to the development of spiritual autobiography. The brief accounts written by Luther and Calvin about their own "conversions" to new theological forms appear not to have encouraged imitations from their initial followers, and were in themselves ambiguous in how normative these reformers expected their personal experiences to be. Only with the emergence of affective pietism in the seventeenth century did the subjective impulse come to be indelibly ingrafted into Protestant religious life.

With its accent on defining religion primarily as an affective and personal phenomenon, this new evangelical pietism proved to be a natural source for the nurturing of an autobiographical tradition, whether in the form of spiritual diaries, conversion narratives, or spiritual autobiographies. The depreciation of the sacraments and the increased importance given to the written word in Protestantism meant that the preferred method of discerning salvation was to be through a language of self that assumed the sacramental function to disclose, through the tangible expression of the language itself, the evidences of an invisible grace. The spiritual diaries of the Puritans, for example, in which the Puritan could examine his or her life for the signs of grace that might indicate election to salvation, gave objective shape to subjective experience and provided "the Puritan substitute for the confessional" in the vacuum left by the elimination of the older penitential system.[19] Although in many ways incomplete and tentative, the spiritual diaries of Puritanism moved conversion out of the psychic realm identified by Bruss and made it fully a product of a retrospective and literary reflection.

There were numerous reasons for keeping a spiritual diary, according to John Beadle, a minister in Barnstone, England, and disciple of the great Puritan divine Thomas Hooker. Beadle published a guide on the subject in 1656, and his instructions demonstrate the close relationship that the Puritan found not only between personal salvation and introspection but also between redemption and retrospection. The primary focus of the spiritual diary, of course, was the author's conversion experience. "Let every man," Beadle urged, "keep a strict account of his effectual calling, and of his age in Christ; and (if it may be) set down the time when, and the place where, and the person by whom he was converted . . . [though] every one cannot relate it, as *Paul* could, in all the circumstances." But the author's task was also more conventionally autobiographical. According to Beadle, spiritual diarists were to record "what times we have lived in, what ministers we have lived under, what callings we were of, what wealth was bestowed upon us, what places of authority and command were committed to us." "I am assured," Beadle continued, "to read a story of our own lives, would be a study (next [to] that of the holy Scripture) as pleasant and profitable as any."[20] In fact, the spiritual diary, argued John Fuller in his preface to Beadle's handbook, was to parallel the actual "diary" of one's lived experience: "There is a book of three leaves thou shouldest read daily to make up this [written] diary; the black leaf of thy own and others' sins with shame and sorrow; the white leaf of God's goodness, mercies with joy and thankfulness; the red leaf of God's judgments felt, feared, threatened, with fear and trembling." Life itself was now a "text" to be read; and in his use of such an analogy, Fuller gave voice to what Margaret Aston termed "the textual consciousness of the age" that was expressed in such telling metaphors.[21] Ideally, suggested Fuller, the spiritual diary was to become a great autobiographical account book, a "divine arithmetic" to which diarists were expected to "[b]ring in your tallies of old, if you look for new mercies to be put upon your account."[22]

There is a facile quality to Fuller's comparison of the spiritual diary to an account ledger that may signify the close association of Puritanism with the emerging merchant class of England, but both Fuller and Beadle identified more divine archetypes for the genre. David, Moses, and the children of Israel, Beadle contended, kept diaries; and the focus of his own text—the biblical book of Numbers—is indicative of his argument that the Exodus event, with its deliverance from slavery, confrontation with temptation, and emphasis on accounting and numbering, provides a narrative prototype for all spiritual diarists. Fuller also found biblical precedent: God himself, Fuller argued, kept a daily account of the creation which had been recorded in the first chapter of Genesis. In fact, Beadle noted, "God himself seems to keep a journal by him of all the care he hath of us, the cost he bestows upon us, and the good things he gives to us. He hath a book of remembrance of every passage of providence that concerns us. And indeed, the Scripture for a great part is little else but a history of his goodness to his people."[23] God, in other words, was the first spiritual diarist, and the Bible was his paradigm for all of the elect to follow.

In finding such precedents in the biblical text for spiritual diary-keeping, Beadle and Fuller were doing more than engaging in an act of creative exegesis; they were contributing to the intertextual reconstruction of what it meant to live an authentically human life. If the Bible was God's own journal, and if human life was to be read in the same way that one would read a text, then the narrative creation of "self" within a spiritual diary was to do nothing more than to mirror the divine and cosmic archetypes. The close relationship between the act of writing and the redemptive activity of God clearly indicates the appropriateness of such an "autobiographical" literary form to the religious conceptions of Protestant pietism.

Whatever the actual source of such a literary form (and for the Puritan mind such biblical models cannot be casually dismissed) the spiritual diary was an exceptionally popular form of Puritan literature. Not only have many diaries themselves survived, but other writings often make mention of their existence and utility in Puritan society. Puritan biographers often noted that such diaries provided them their primary source material, although the more common fate of the diaries (sometimes after their use by a pious biographer) was destruction following the death of the subject.[24] "[I]f I should die before I have committed this book to the flames," wrote Joseph Green, the minister in Salem Village, Massachusetts, "I give leave to my nearest relation to look over it; but I give strict charge to them not to expose it to the view of any. And it is my will that this book be viewed by none unless by one person which is nearest related to me." Honesty, not modesty, provided the reasoning behind such sentiments. After making clear his request for privacy, Green immediately added, "now I pray God to help me write sincerely[,] humbly, and without any ostentation."[25] Only by protecting their privacy could diarists hope to examine candidly the "black leaf" of which Fuller wrote, and thus engage the totality of their own sinfulness and struggle against doubt.

Here was the discursive innovation in Anglo-Protestantism wrought by Puritanism. In the private "confessional" of the diary, the diarist became both penitent and confessor; his or her life became the stage for the great drama of salvation, a microcosm of the macrocosmic battle between God and Satan. If the infusion of divine grace could be conceived as a moment of affective enlightenment, then it could be something that entered into the domain of history and thus temporally located within the life of the individual. Personal history was transformed into sacred history, and "God's great plot" of redemption, as the Reverend Thomas Shepard of Cambridge, Massachusetts, termed it in his spiritual diary, became tangible in the contemplation of one's own life.[26] Sin, doubt, and despair were not merely psychic states but objective reality; their inward presence was demonstrated by the events and circumstances of one's outward life and could be expressed in narrative form. In similar manner, one could search the "white leaf" of God's tangible mercies for signs of election and salvation. In his or her quest for the assurance of salvation, the individual diarist thus typified the redemptive task of all Christians.

The diary, however, remained an intensely personal document. No matter how typical the quest for salvation and assurance might be, no matter how similar one's life might appear to that of another, these things were not intended for public consumption through the pages of the diary. The spiritual diaries that have survived from the Puritan era did so by accident or in express contradiction to the wishes of their authors. Whatever helps the diary might offer were intended only as an aid to the author, not as a model for others. The autobiographical act, it might be argued, was an accident of the diurnal process, not its substance; and like the life they recorded, they were, by their nature as daily documents, always in process, unfinished and incomplete.

Only with the introduction of the oral relation as a condition of church membership did autobiographical activity begin to assume both a personal closure and a communal acknowledgment and appropriation in Puritanism. Beginning in the middle of the seventeenth century, the Puritan churches in the Massachusetts Bay Colony began to require the relation of one's conversion experience as a necessary qualification for individual church membership and communally as the foundation for any new congregations. What had been (and continued to be) in the diaries personal and private now became institutional and public. Although there remained an impermanence and unfinished quality in these expressions—most profoundly exemplified in the fact that they were conceived and executed primarily as oral accounts—the relations placed the subjective impulse at the very heart of Puritan ecclesiastical life.

The foundations for the use of such oral relations is not clear, although they were being used sporadically at least as early as the 1630s. In 1648, the ministers who drew up the Cambridge Platform officially sanctioned and institutionalized the practice by requiring that all prospective church members orally deliver a "personal and public confession, and declaring of God's manner of working upon the soul" prior to the granting of membership status and admission to the sacraments.[27] For at least a generation, and in some locales even longer, this autobiographical activity was the foundation of ecclesiastical polity and practice in New England's Congregational churches.

There were inherent tensions, however, in this demand to give a narrative of conversion that was both "personal and public." By assuming such a public function, conversion could not be regarded as merely a psychic or even a personal phenomenon. It now involved the convert, the auditors, and, by extension, the entire community in the construction of a new discursive reality that was founded upon the ability of the convert to speak of conversion in a way that could receive the approbation of congregation and community. As Patricia Caldwell observed in her superb analysis of the oral relations, the speaker was charged to deliver "in his or her own words" a "living experience of the heart," while the audience was charged with "a spiritual act—of hearing, of rendering the 'judgment of charity,' and of receiving (sometimes rejecting) a 'living stone' for the temple."[28] Although the autobiographical intent of the relations was—like that of the diaries—almost circumstantial, the relations became significant discursive sites from which the converts created themselves and structured their experiences through narrative. Conversion, in the relations, became more than a constant introspection for the signs of grace in the manner of the spiritual diaries. By demanding some degree of narrated retrospection, the oral relations externalized the Puritan quest for the signs of election and rendered conversion, in the words of Caldwell, a "literary judgment."[29]

Although Puritanism was unable to sustain the requirement of oral relations, it heralded the emergence of autobiography as a literary form particularly suited to pietistic life and practice. Beset by the necessities of biology in the face of their refusal to abandon infant baptism as a valid sacramental sign of membership in the church, Puritanism quietly discarded the use of the relations for all intents and purposes when they opened church membership to the baptized but unconverted children of unconverted parents.[30] The revival of the ecclesiastical use of oral relations within the evangelical tradition may be traced in part to Jonathan Edwards, who, although unsuccessful in attempting to reinstate the use of oral relation in his own parish, made conversion narratives an important part of his theological dissection of the conversion experience.

Edwards stands as the great mediating figure between Puritanism and evangelicalism, and his explorations of conversion and the "religious affections" exercised great influence during the time when the stream of Puritan piety was beginning to flow into evangelical channels. Although his predecessor in the pulpit of the Northampton, Massachusetts, Congregational Church—his own grandfather Solomon Stoddard—had discarded the use of oral relations, Edwards began to reconsider their significance when the first of a series of religious awakenings occurred during his ministry. Following years of stagnant interest in religious matters, Edwards claimed, many members of his congregation suddenly, and often dramatically, experienced conversion during the winter of 1734–35, and the resultant "revival" spread rapidly throughout the frontier communities of the Connecticut River Valley, foreshadowing the great revival of the 1740s that was to become New England's "Great Awakening." In many ways a champion of the traditional order of the Congregational Way, Edwards nonetheless emerged as a leading spokesperson and key defender of the more affective forms of piety that were unleashed during the awakenings.

Promotion of affective conversion was Edwards's chief aim as pastor, and in his account of the 1734–35 awakening he commented, "There is no one thing I know of, that God has made such a means of promoting his work amongst us, as the news of others' conversion[s]."[31] To this end, Edwards experimented with using the conversion accounts of certain of his parishioners as propagandistic tools to defend both the awakening and the sometimes excessive physical and emotional forms that conversion took. While the accounts that Edwards employed for his apologia of the revival were not autobiographical in the strict sense of the term, they do link the Puritan oral relations with the later evangelical spiritual autobiographies. In the words of Daniel Shea, Edwards's "presentations of spiritual biography" became for later evangelicals "essential history" in the sense that the paradigms of conversion he presented became the standard form for later evangelical conversion.[32]

In his first defense of the awakening, entitled *A Faithful Narrative of the Surprising Work of God,* Edwards used the conversion accounts of two female parishioners: A young woman named Abigail Hutchinson, who had died shortly after her conversion, and Phebe Bartlet, a four-year-old child. Edwards intended this work to be both a descriptive and an analytical assessment of the revival, and so he offered not only a recapitulation of the events of the awakening, but also a theological exegesis of the experience of conversion. The accounts of Hutchinson and Bartlet were his "case studies," which were based on his own personal interviews and close acquaintance with the subjects and were intended to be "two particular instances" selectively chosen in order "to give a clearer idea of the nature and manner of the operations of God's Spirit" in the experience of conversion.[33] In fact, they were perhaps too particular; supporters of the revival found in the accounts of Hutchinson and Bartlet simplistic models of conversion that avoided the subtleties, nuances, and particularities that Edwards himself cautioned were always present in genuine conversions. The fact that Hutchinson was a young woman dying from some unnamed disease, coupled with the precociousness of the four-year-old Bartlet, gave both accounts a pathological and, at least in the case of Hutchinson, morbid texture, and led to the accusation by both contemporary opponents and more recent scholars that Edwards purposely chose the most dramatic examples of conversion he could find.[34] Edwards tried in subsequent writings to defuse the controversy by insisting that the work of grace could not be limited to set patterns or absolute procedures, arguing that "[e]xperience plainly shows, that God's Spirit is unsearchable and untraceable, in some of the best of Christians, in the method of his operations, in their conversion," but his protestations in the long run proved "less effective than the models he had himself set up."[35]

Edwards subsequently attempted to counter the emotional intensity of Hutchinson's and Bartlet's accounts by next employing in another defense of the revivals the conversion account of his wife, Sarah Pierpont Edwards. If Hutchinson and Bartlet proved too "particular," Sarah's narrative in the hands of her husband was transformed into an anonymous account that mythologized and idealized its subject for Edwards's own polemic purposes. Edwards purposely destroyed the historical uniqueness of Sarah's account by deleting all clues that might betray the identity, even the sex, of his subject, noting only that her conversion took place apart from either the "enthusiastical season" of the revival or "that enthusiastical town of Northampton." Aside from these few ambiguous signs, Edwards kept the account totally detached from specific events. In her husband's hands, Sarah's account in fact lapses into a lyrical paean on the ecstasy of an almost mystical spiral of religious experience from joy to doubt to joy again, coming closer and closer in each revolution to "a pure delight that fed and satisfied the soul . . . without being in any trance, or being at all deprived of the exercise of the bodily senses."[36]

Like the Greco-Roman biographers, Edwards sought to discover the transcendent in the mundane, the universal within the particular, but his redaction of Sarah's narrative was a relative failure. If conversion was an eruption of the eternal into history, then its evidences could not be so easily dehistoricized. For a final time, however, Edwards attempted to use a conversion narrative to support his theological understanding of conversion when his daughter's fiancé, a young missionary named David Brainerd, succumbed to tuberculosis in the Edwards household and left Edwards in charge of his diaries and journals.

The use of Brainerd's diaries offered Edwards some definite advantages over the narratives of Hutchinson, Bartlet, and Sarah. In contrast to the three earlier accounts, Edwards for the first time possessed a usable account by a male convert rather than a female whose emotional estate might provide additional ammunition for his opponents. Further, Brainerd's religious dedication had been proven by his missionary efforts among Native Americans when a settled parochial ministry was closed to him; he was a seasoned adult convert who had known and heroically endured adversity and discouragement. Edwards did not need to cloak Brainerd's account under the generic descriptions he had used in Sarah's narrative; indeed, Brainerd's devotion to the ministry could be used to Edwards's advantage. Finally, Brainerd's piety had been formed independently of Edwards's tutelage and his narrative was not the product of Edwards but an independent account. Edwards could present Brainerd essentially in Brainerd's own words. Whatever hopes Edwards may have entertained for the acceptance of this work were no doubt wildly exceeded: *The Life of David Brainerd* became an evangelical devotional classic and was Edwards's most popular and most reprinted work.[37]

Even with Brainerd's diaries at hand, however, there were problems with Edwards's use of Brainerd's conversion account. Dismissed from Yale College because of alleged "enthusiasm" and conflict with his tutor, Brainerd's diaries demonstrated in places an excessive religious melancholy that could provide enemies of the revival with further cause for reproach. Edwards was forced to depreciate the entire incident at Yale and to restructure and palliate sections that suggested religious depression, but his *exemplum* could never be the idealized presentation that had marked Greco-Roman and medieval Christian biography. Like the earlier Puritans and the later evangelicals, conversion became, for Edwards, a problem of discourse, where the demands of history clashed with traditional religious ideology. The "historical" Brainerd could not always be easily reconciled with the Brainerd of Edwards's theological model. It is little wonder that Edwards's account of his own conversion, which also did not fit the general pattern he struggled to articulate in his theoretical works, was never published during his lifetime.[38]

Edwards's attempts to use conversion narratives for theological ends only led to increased criticism from his opponents and displayed the tension between religious ideal and historical verity that would become a significant expression in later evangelical accounts. For better or worse, the conversion narratives of Hutchinson, Bartlet, and Brainerd came to define the parameters of a very affective style of conversion for most later evangelicals who looked to Edwards's theological and apologetic works as foundations for their own beliefs and practices. The "manifestation" of conversion that Edwards tried so carefully to circumscribe in the tangible examples he presented provided a paradigm of narrative catharsis through which later evangelicals would construct themselves as both subjects and objects of historical consciousness.

Ironically, Edwards's attempts to reimpose the requirement of oral relations on his Northampton congregation cost him his pulpit and ended his career as a revivalist, but a revival of the practice of delivering an oral relation to gain church membership seems to have been renewed at about the time of Edwards's death and no doubt helped to precipitate the formation of an autobiographical tradition among evangelicals.[39] While some evangelical groups, such as the Presbyterians, avoided making the ability to relate a conversion experience a prerequisite for church membership, other traditions employed a form of narrative scrutiny not dissimilar to the Puritan practice of visible sainthood. As early as the 1760s, the Separate Baptists moving into Virginia quarreled over the issue of oral relations with the Regular Baptists already settled there, complaining "of the Regulars not being *strict enough in receiving experiences,* when persons made application to their churches for baptism, or in order to become church members."[40] Some twenty years later, Barton Stone commented on the continuing popularity and ecclesiastical utility of such narratives in Baptist life. As a young man, Stone first encountered evangelicalism through a small Baptist community that had been gathered near his Virginia home, and his memories of the group focused on the conversion narratives he heard:

> I was a constant attendant, and was particularly interested to hear the converts giving in their experience. Of their conviction and great distress for sin, they were

very particular in giving an account, and how and when they obtained deliverance from their burdens. Some were delivered by a dream, a vision, or some uncommon appearance of light—some by a voice spoken to them, "Thy sins are forgiven thee"—and others by seeing the Saviour with their natural eyes. Such experiences were considered good by the church, and the subjects of them were received for baptism, and into full fellowship.[41]

Use of conversion narratives to determine fitness for church membership was not limited to either Baptists in the South or the Separates. Ray Potter described in his autobiography his own only partially successful experience in 1812 when he had to give an oral account of his conversion in order to join a Freewill Baptist congregation in Rhode Island. By the middle of the nineteenth century, the most prominent interpreter of American religion could remark, "There may be difference of opinion among truly evangelical Christians respecting the amount of evidence of conversion necessary, [but] . . . with few exceptions all expect some evidence in every candidate for admission to the Church and participation in its most precious privileges; and such evidence, too, as induces the belief that, as the Scriptures express it, [the convert] has 'passed from death unto life.'"[42]

Such documentary evidence points to the centrality of conversion discourse within evangelical Protestantism. Even when such testimonies were not required in order to join as full members of a church or congregation, opportunities to hear and deliver such accounts were frequent and were a common characteristic of many evangelical gatherings. Abner Chase recounted that during one Methodist class meeting, "At the very commencement of the meeting, an awful power and influence rested upon the congregation. Singing, prayer, exhortation, and the relation of Christian experience, were continued for some time." Such public testimonies were powerful contributions to the affective intent of the service. "[A]lmost every heart seemed to be melted or moved," Chase recalled. "Tears flowed freely from many eyes unused to weeping; sobs and sighs were heard in almost every part of the house." At a later "love-feast, on sabbath morning," Chase noted, "there were shouts of praise to God, mingled with the relation of Christian experience, in which many were ready and even anxious to bear a part." Even the required testimonies of the Baptists could produce similarly emotional effects. "When the churches held conference to receive members," observed one early Baptist history, "the congregation would draw up in such crowds, as they would tread one on another, anxious to hear the experiences of their neighbors and families. And while the candidates were relating their experience, the audience would be in floods of tears, and some almost convulsed, while their children, companions, and friends were relating their conversion. And several declared this was the means of their conviction." Whether regulated and serving ecclesiastical ends or thoroughly spontaneous, conversion testimonies were more than individual exercises of personal piety; they were important expressions of evangelical corporate life that could be irrepressible. "In the public assembly, even when there was no liberty given," wrote the Freewill Baptist David Marks, "feeling the Lord required it, I was frequent in my testimonies."[43]

Marks's compulsion provides an insight into the subjective impulse of early evangelicalism. Even when the narration of conversion served no practical ecclesiastical ends, evangelicals recognized in the experience of conversion an impetus that both compelled and vindicated their autobiographical expression. If the Puritans had struggled with the issues of self-expression in their brief oral relations, these tensions were intensified in evangelical spiritual autobiographies that could not even make the claim that they provided the necessary evidence to gain church membership. In the process, however, the spiritual autobiography emerged as a site where the author no longer verified conversion, but where conversion justified the self.

According to the argument of one of the pioneers of autobiographical criticism, autobiography becomes possible only within the framework of "a cultural revolution"—at that moment when human beings "have emerged from the mythic framework of traditional teachings and . . . entered into the perilous domain of history." Similarly, Karl J. Weintraub argued that "the autobiographic genre took in its full dimension and richness when Western Man acquired a thoroughly historical understanding of his existence."[44] The emergence of a modern historical consciousness was certainly fundamental for the formulation of the autobiographical genre, although recent critics have challenged the naive notion that autobiography has to align itself with historical veracity any more than any other genre (even including fiction). Still, the tension between history and myth was a crucial one for evangelicals, whose forays into the autobiographical field presented them with a host of new problems. Although the biographies of heroes, the martyrologies, and the hagiographies of the ancient and medieval worlds were expected to be "fictive" to a large degree, autobiography, in most definitions of the term, was supposed to reflect better the "truth" of a person's life. In order to impose some meaning on the historical "facts" of one's existence, however, the autobiographer continued to confront the need to mythologize her narrative in order to supply it with a meaning beyond the personal.

Evangelical spiritual autobiographers obviously did not use the terminology of history and myth to describe their literary endeavors, but it was precisely at the juncture between these two ways of understanding and shaping reality that spiritual autobiography achieved its authority as a site of evangelical discourse. If history involved the recognition of temporality and change, myth referred to the immutable and eternal, presenting the archetypes and exemplary patterns into which the events of history needed to be placed in order to gain meaning. As ontological categories, Mircea Eliade argues, myth is thus the more powerful form of modeling reality since it points to the enduring rather than the ephemeral. Myth, according to Eliade's understanding, "*reveals* something as having been *fully manifested,* and this manifestation is at the same time *creative* and *exemplary,* since it is the foundation of a structure of reality as well as a kind of human behavior. A myth always narrates something as having *really happened.* . . . Myths reveal the structure of reality . . . they disclose the *true* stories, concern themselves with the *realities.*"[45]

That these two components, history and myth, formed the essence of evangelical spiritual autobiography can be seen in the model presented by Charles Giles. The peculiarities of time and circumstance—what Giles referred to as the "account of the responsible part acted by the person himself; [and] the treatment he has received from his fellow-men"—composed the historical element of the spiritual autobiography, and so evangelicals, living in the age of the "subjective impulse," understood themselves to be both subjects and objects of history. More significant to the production of a spiritual autobiography, however, was the mythic pattern or model into which such transitory historical circumstances could be fitted in order to discern their timeless meaning and significance. When the nineteenth-century spiritual autobiographer struggled to articulate himself as a historical being, it was the mythic pattern of conversion—"his Christian experience; and how Providence has attended him from year to year," according to Giles—that validated his effort. Only insofar as the presentation of an individual life disclosed this immutable model—or only insofar as it could be made to conform to such—did the spiritual autobiography perform its discursive task.

Although the specific circumstances differed from individual to individual, aligning one's life with the proper pattern prevented its submergence into what Eliade termed "the terror of history."[46] For most evangelical spiritual autobiographers, such alignment was not a conscious effort; indeed, in their descriptions, one might be tempted to argue that the pattern often came seeking them instead. John Hudson, a Methodist, reported an unexpected parallelism between his life and the pattern of conversion presented through scripture and sermon. "The minister took his text from 'Is thy heart right?' As he advanced in his discourse, it appeared as if he knew all the facts of my history. . . . At one point of his sermon, the preacher, holding the candle in his hand, and moving two or three paces in the direction of where I sat, and repeating, Is *thy* heart right? appeared to say to me: 'Thou art the man.'" In addition to the patterns presented from the biblical text or the pulpit, many evangelicals cited analogues discovered in the experiences of others, even when they disclaimed any prior knowledge of the conventional process of conversion. "Thinking my distress singular," recounted Baptist autobiographer Henry Holcombe, "I was agreeably surprised to find . . . [that the experiences of former companions] had been of a similar nature."[47]

Whatever the source of the model of conversion, nowhere was the tension between history and myth more pronounced than in their spiritual autobiographies. Here evangelicals struggled with the exigencies of their profane existence and the demands of the mythic model. On one level, their autobiographic movement was through physical space and historical time, marked by references to specific places, dates, and interaction with other individuals. On a deeper level, however, this same movement was through a space and time sacralized by the presence of conversion. The very possibility of autobiographic activity established a uniqueness that prevented the reduction of the subject to an ideal type, yet the focus on conversion represented a participation in and a recapitulation of the transhistorical redemptive activity of God. If the text of the conversion narrative was the enunciative site from which the convert could speak with authority, it was also the location from which the convert contended between these opposing forces.

In short, the spiritual autobiographies of early evangelicals were profoundly modernist texts because the central problem with which they struggled—the problem of the self as both the maker and object of history—was a profoundly modernist problem. If the spiritual autobiographer was aware of the need to mold her life into an acceptable pattern of conversion, she was also aware of her existence as a historical being. This "historical self" was not easily conformed to the "mythic self," and so the convert who spoke from the site of the autobiographical text faced a fundamental dilemma: the paradox of the self.

CHAPTER THREE

THE PARADOX OF
THE SELF

*There is a difficulty attending this kind of writing, which cannot well
be avoided; that is of saying I, so often; the author having himself
constantly in view, while writing upon the subject.*

—*Elias Smith, 1816*

The issue of selfhood haunted evangelical autobiographies. Although never fully defined, the self involved
spiritual autobiographers in a fundamental paradox that
they often recognized but were unable to eliminate. According to their theology, conversion implied a type of
negation or overcoming of self; yet, as Elias Smith con-
fessed, the self was in fact more fully asserted—even created—through the narrative process. Despite protests to
the contrary, the central character of any conversion account, spiritual diary, or spiritual autobiography was the
convert, not God. The issue of the self, particularly the
creation of self and the structuring of personal identity,
formed the very center of this genre of religious literature,
but at the heart of the evangelical conversion experience
was a profound ambivalence of self. The problem, as authors such as Smith were forced to concede, was the "I."

The evangelical morphology of conversion required

that converts speak a language of self-negation, but evangelical autobiographers struggled with the irony that the more they spoke the expected language, the more self-focused and even self-creative their narratives became. The Methodist Abner Chase gave eloquent expression to this dilemma in his 1846 spiritual autobiography, which had been originally serialized in the *Northern Christian Advocate.* At the beginning of his narrative, Chase offered the odd disclaimer that even though he was writing his autobiography, "I will here state that I shall say as little of myself in these sketches as consistently I can, but shall feel bound occasionally to glance at my own experience." The express intent of the work, despite its attention to Chase's own experiences, was altruistic and prescriptive: To present for the reader "the sum total of the ground or condition of the justification of the sinner, namely repentance toward God, and faith toward our Lord Jesus Christ." Chase's own experiences would be merely exemplary, to direct the reader toward this ultimate goal. "[W]hat more is required or necessary," Chase asked rhetorically, "than that a man should see and feel that he is a sinner, lost and undone—that there is no help in himself—and that he then throw himself upon the promises of God, as given in the gospel, and embrace Christ by faith, as the great atoning sacrifice for sin?"[1]

The paradox, as Chase discovered, was in the fact that in presenting himself as a model of such self-abnegation, he was in fact asserting himself all the more. Of his own conversion, Chase wrote, "I found power by faith to lay hold, as I had never done before, upon the promises of the gospel," but was compelled immediately to ask the indulgence of his readers—"If my readers will excuse this detail of my own experience, perhaps I shall not tax their patience so heavily again." But if his own self-presentation was a tax levied upon his readers, Chase could not help but assess them repeatedly, and the narrative records Chase's progressive recognition of this problem. "When I commenced these sketches," he finally lamented, "I thought and stated that I should say as little of myself as consistently I could, and I still wish to do so. But I find as I proceed that 'I' must be written much oftener than was at first intended, or the circumstances cannot be stated which I wish to give."[2]

Chase's frustrations and confusions articulated the paradox of the self that evangelical spiritual autobiographers encountered. The language of conversion pressed them to speak of self-annihilation, but in speaking thus they counteracted the very intent of such discourse. The self they encountered in their narratives was not simply "the modern word for 'soul'" as John Morris described it; these two terms are indicative of fundamentally different ways of understanding the meaning of human existence.[3] Although evangelical autobiographers used a very traditional language in describing their conversions, the orthodoxy of their language could not disguise the struggle for selfhood that was waged because of, and sometimes in spite of, the discursive requirements.

Etymologically, Hayden White reminds us, "the word *discourse* ... suggests a movement 'back and forth' or a 'running to and fro.'" Thus, according to White, "A discourse moves 'to and fro' between received encodations of experience and the clutter of phenomena which refuses incorporation into conventionalized notions of 'reality,' 'truth,' or 'possibility.' ... Discourse, in a word, is quintessentially a *mediative* enterprise."[4] To read conversion as a discursive trope that mediates between the self-creativity of the autobiographical act and the self-annihilation demanded by the language of Protestant pietism is to recognize that evangelical spiritual autobiographies cannot be dismissed as merely imitative accounts controlled by exterior conventions. The morphology of conversion, no matter how much evangelicals utilized it, carried a function far beyond that of simple repetition or affectation. Simply put, the language of conversion allowed the pietist to speak about the self at a time when changing attitudes about individuality and personal identity were beginning to blur traditional distinctions and increase ambiguities.

Since at least the time of René Descartes in the early seventeenth century, the ancient Christian notion of the embodied soul had been slowly giving way to a more modern conception of the self as a thinking, experiencing, and more autonomous entity. The traditional theological discourse of Christianity conceived of human identity as fundamentally a combination of corporeal body and incorporeal soul. Against both Neoplatonic speculation and Gnostic conceptions, Christian doctrine held that the soul was not a fallen spark of divinity, but nonetheless composed the spiritual essence of human life that distinguished human beings from other created life forms. Humanity was the crown of creation because human beings possessed both a material body (unlike the angels) and a spiritual form—the soul—that was absent in animals. As the Fourth Lateran Council would later state the matter in its official condemnation of the quasi-Gnostic Albigensian sect, God "by His almighty power from the beginning of time made at once . . . out of nothing both orders of creatures, the spiritual and the corporeal, that is, the angelic and the earthly, and then . . . the human creature, who as it were shares in both orders, being composed of spirit and body."[5]

Early Christianity generally followed Greek philosophy in defining the soul (Greek: *psyche*) as a substantial form, separable from the body, and the seat of volition and rationality. Ascribing immortality to the soul posed a more difficult problem, since for the Christian it implied only the soul's survival after death and not its preexistence. Christian apologists explained that the soul was not by nature immortal, but could become such through the power of the resurrection of Christ.[6] This possibility of immortality, however, was vitally important since it connected the human soul to divinity. In the Eastern churches, theologians read this "likeness" of the soul to the divine nature as proof of the possibility of human deification through the power of the incarnation of God in Jesus; as Athanasius of Alexandria expressed it in his treatise on the incarnation, "he was made man that we might be made God."[7] Speculation on the soul was thus oriented toward the future; salvation ultimately encompassed the reunification of the body with its animating force (the soul) in the resurrection.

Western Christians, on the other hand, held a more juridical understanding of salvation. The soul became the focus of a process of redemption based on a soteriology of "satisfaction" for human sin. The incarnation of Christ and the resurrection of the body were still essential components in Western theology, of course, but their functions received a slightly different significance within the process of human salvation. The classic Western counterpart to Athanasius's treatise was Anselm's essay entitled "Why God Became Man." According to Anselm, "without satisfaction, that is, without the willing payment of man's debt, God cannot remit sin unpunished . . . [and] while no one save God can make it [satisfaction] and no one save man ought to make it, it is necessary for a God-Man to make it."[8] Salvation was thus a moral problem, made possible initially through the incarnation, but generally applied through participation in the sacraments that had been instituted by Christ for the remission of sins. Through the grace received in baptism and continued through the sacraments of penance and the Eucharist, God granted forgiveness and reconciliation to individuals. This redemptive process was complete only after death, when the soul, which survived death (thus ensuring the retention of the "matter and memory of the same human being," according to Tertullian), was reunited with the body in the resurrection, and both the material and spiritual components that defined humanity were restored to their full and divinely intended integrity.[9]

In both East and West, theologians agreed that the intuitive inclination of the soul was toward heavenly things. As the spiritual constituent of human life, the soul represented that which, in its uncorrupted state, desired reintegration with the divine. "Even deceived by its adversary," argued Tertullian, the soul "remembers its Author, His goodness and law, its own end, and its adversary. Is it so extraordinary, then, if, being a gift of God, it proclaims the same things which God has given to His own people to know?" Gregory of Nyssa associated the soul—as the image of God in human beings—with its divine archetype and argued that "[s]ince all nature is attracted to what is related to it and a human being is somehow related to God, containing within himself imitations of the archetype, the soul is necessarily attracted to the divine and related to it."[10] Given this line of reasoning, the soul thus might be understood as existing in a state of alienation from its true essence, if not for the total sum of human life (that is, between birth and death but prior to the resurrection), then at least prior to one's "rebirth" at the font of baptism. Although, against gnosticism, Christian theology would assert that such alienation was never complete (the "flesh" was corrupted but not totally evil), salvation or deification enabled the soul to overcome this alienation from its divine source. "[T]rue religion," observed Augustine, "is that by which the soul binds itself again to the one and only God and reconciles itself to Him from whom it had torn itself away, as it were, by sin."[11] With God himself, the soul shared the divine characteristics of spirit, immortality, and rationality; it was a gift of God, the most divinized aspect of the human constitution, created by God and vouchsafed to unworthy mortals. Thus, it was toward the soul that salvation was directed; the salvation of one's immortal soul was the goal of the Christian and the task of the Church.

Despite the orientation of the soul toward its divine archetype, however, early and medieval theologians recognized that the interior life of the Christian remained one of struggle, doubt, and moral deficiency. "As for me, when I deliberated upon serving the Lord my God, as I had long planned to do," Augustine wrote in the clearest expression of this inner tension, "it was myself who willed it and I myself who did not will it. It was I myself. I neither willed it completely, nor did I refrain completely from willing it. Therefore, I was at war within myself, and I was laid waste by myself."[12] Augustine's war within himself depicts the problematic nature of human autonomy that made the self—to adopt an anachronistic label—a more troublesome entity than the divinized soul. As an essential expression of human nature, the self was the seat of pride, egotism, and conceit and thus stood opposed to the surrender to the divine call and return to its source. Salvation might satisfy the longing of the soul toward God, but it could come only with the renunciation of the self. If the self was not more "secular" than the soul, certainly it was more problematic.[13]

An alternative way of describing this division of the human being was to adopt the Pauline distinction between the "natural man" and the new creation in Christ, a distinction that governed the Christian vision of self and society during late antiquity and the early Middle Ages. As a part of nature, human beings shared in the current fallen and chaotic state of nature which had to be overcome in order for the individual to achieve salvation. For Paul, this was accomplished through the mystery of being "in Christ"; for the medieval Western Church, the reality of this transformation of the human being from the natural to the sacralized state was achieved through the sacrament of baptism. It was through baptism that the individual "divested himself of his natural humanity, his *humanitas,* and . . . [became] a participant of the divine attributes themselves."[14]

The effects of baptism were not limited, however, to the private transformation of one's inner being; with the development of the concept of the *corpus christianum* in the early Middle Ages, baptism also signaled one's incorporation into the larger Christian social order. According to the Christian political theory, the status of any society, as a corporate "body," paralleled that of the human individual and thus existed in either a natural or a Christian state. If nature was the realm of human equity, it was also the fallen realm of chaos; only a Christian society was properly ordered according to divine plan and was necessarily hierarchical. By "virtue of his baptism and the consequential incorporation into the Church," Walter Ullmann explained, the individual gave his implicit approval to this hierarchical system and thus retained "no autonomous character" in medieval society.[15]

The absorption of the individual self into the corporate whole in medieval society can, of course, be easily overdrawn. The practical realities of social forms such as feudalism recognized certain contractual obligations between individuals that political philosophy did not. In fact, the Church itself contributed to the recovery of "the individual in his natural state" in its acceptance of Aristotelian philosophy in the thirteenth century. Thomas Aquinas's baptism of Aristotle into the medieval Christian constitution allowed for a "double ordering of things" that made room for both the natural and the supernatural order in the construction of society.[16] Even then, however, there existed a tension between the individual as political citizen and the individual as Christian subject, a tension that retained its hold on the Western political imagination until the intellectual revolutions of the seventeenth and eighteenth centuries remodeled social theory on the basis of consent rather than a divinely mandated hierarchy.

Renewed attention to the autonomous self first appeared under the guise of Christian humanism during the period of the Renaissance. The humanists reappropriated the Augustinian dilemma "as a paradigm for the inner life,"[17] and so expanded the subjectivist impulse found in *Confessions* into a decidedly different, and more modern, way of conceiving what it meant to be human. The new intellectual, political, and religious movements that followed in the wake of the Renaissance—Protestantism, the Enlightenment, Pietism, the rise of democracy and capitalism—all turned their attention at one time or another to the issue of the self. The human being was increasingly defined as an autonomous entity invested with volitional power within both religious and social affairs and not as an embodied soul longing for reintegration with the divine. The individual was freed from the demands of the traditional Christian faith and freed likewise from the demands of the corporate state unless one chose to "voluntarily" place oneself within the "covenant" of the Church or within the "contract" of society. Although human beings still lived their lives within political, religious, and economic communities, more and more these communities came to be defined as aggregates of individuals rather than truly corporate structures.

If Renaissance humanism, infused with a renewed appreciation of Augustinian introspection, provided an important foundation for the disintegration of the corporate emphasis of medieval Catholicism and the development of modern notions of the autonomous self, Protestantism provided the primary structure in which this idea took definitive shape. On the one hand, magisterial Protestantism—the Protestantism of Luther, Bucer, Zwingli, Bullinger, Calvin, and their colleagues—had no intention of dismantling the communal focus of traditional Catholicism. Martin Luther's "Address to the German Nobility" in 1520 assumed the continued existence of a coherent Christendom even while he argued strenuously against its religious hierarchy. Likewise, Martin Bucer in Strasbourg, Ulrich Zwingli and Henrich Bullinger in Zurich, and most especially John Calvin in Geneva organized reformed Christian societies, not just individual congregations. Protestantism was to be a reform of Christendom, not a rejection of it. On the other hand, the essential aspects in the development of the concept of the modern autonomous self received the approbation of Protestant theology and practice. In the Protestant accent on the necessity of the individual to stand alone before God, unable ultimately to depend upon the benefits of the sacraments, the priesthood, or the institutional Church, Protestantism planted the seeds of its own theological and social fragmentation.

Magisterial Protestantism generally resisted the emergence of the modern concept of self, although the Reformers provided important theoretical foundations for modern autonomy. Both Luther and Calvin left "autobiographical" accounts of their crises of faith, but neither seems to have considered their inward turmoil normative for the Christian life. Further, in Luther's refusal to recognize a distinction between a "religious" and a "secular" class, and in the idea of individual "calling" and what Max Weber labeled the "worldly asceticism" of Calvinist theology, both Reformers gave expression to the "affirmation of ordinary life" that Charles Taylor has identified as part of the modernist concept of self.[18] In his *Institutes of the Christian Religion,* Calvin had argued that a "clear and complete knowledge of God" was impossible without "a corresponding knowledge of ourselves," but this was not due to any idea that knowledge of the self provided an affirmation of the self. Rather, knowledge of the self, for Calvin, would lead to "the feeling of our own ignorance, vanity, poverty, infirmity, and . . . depravity and corruption," thus providing the starkest of contrasts wherein might be glimpsed "the true light of wisdom, sound virtue, full abundance of every good, and purity and righteousness" that "rest in the Lord alone." In other words, the proper contemplation of human nature should lead one to recognize the emptiness of self and need for divine assistance. "[W]e cannot seriously aspire to [God] before we begin to become displeased with ourselves," wrote Calvin.[19]

The various forms of Protestant pietism that arose in the seventeenth and eighteenth centuries took to heart Calvin's examination of and displeasure with the self. According to the Puritan minister Thomas Shepard, "the saving knowledge of Christ is dependent upon the sensible knowledge of a man's self"; but, like Calvin, Shepard understood that the true value of such self-knowledge was only in its ability to confirm the misdirection of human concern toward things mundane instead of things transcendent. "All the good things a wicked man doth are for himself," noted Shepard, "either for self-credit or self-ease, or self-content, or self-safety; he sleeps, prays, hears, speaks, professeth for himself alone; hence acting always for himself, he committeth the highest degree of idolatry."[20] Pietistic theology asserted that true salvation implied the negation or extinction of self, or in personal "humiliation," to adopt the term favored by many theologians. In this theological sense, humiliation meant more than just the cultivation of an attitude of pious humility; it was a total emptying of self. "You must be empty, if ever Christ fill you," wrote the influential Puritan divine Thomas Hooker in his treatise on humiliation; "you must be nothing, if you would have Christ all in all to you." A century later, Jonathan Edwards could still maintain that "[e]vangelical humiliation is a sense that a Christian has of his own utter insufficiency, despicableness, and odiousness, with an answerable frame of heart."[21] But iconoclasm requires an icon, and in their need to search themselves in order to deny themselves, pietists had to first imagine themselves. The self, in other words, had to be objectified in order to speak about it in conversionist discourse, paradoxically defeating the intended reason that one spoke the discourse in the first place.[22]

As Sacvan Bercovitch noted in his study of the American Puritan concept of self, the Puritan examination of self for religious benefit was hopelessly incongruous. Humiliation and self-effacement were strategies to construct rather than eliminate the self, creating, in Bercovitch's words, "the profound Puritan ambivalence towards selfhood." Like Augustine, the Puritan was forced into a "Self Civil War" wherein he was "driven by self-loathing to Christ and forced back to himself by the recognition that his labors are an assertion of what he loathes." Offering a testimony of grace such as an oral relation thus posed a dilemma for the Puritan. "The same

'I' that once could not believe was the sole reliable witness—witness, judge, and historian—of the Lord's victory," explained Bercovitch; "the force of I-ness is transparent in the violent vocabulary of self-abhorrence."[23] Conversion, although the fundamental goal of Puritanism, was unattainable except by attention to the self—the very thing that the Puritan was supposed to despise the most and seek to overcome.

Even when the morphology of conversion appears to dominate the production of a narrative, such as in the Puritan oral relations, the "unruly" character of the self intervened to complicate their deceptive simplicity. In other words, the very existence of any "autobiographical action" established a uniqueness of self that prevented the reduction of the subject to an ideal type (on the order of the medieval hagiographies) no matter how conventional or authoritative the language of conversion it presented. In fact, surviving relations are not the confident rehearsals of the conversion morphology presumed by previous scholars, but are uncertain, tentative, and ambivalent accounts in which converts struggled, and often failed, to locate their own experiences within the models proposed by the theologians. The morphologies often proved unhelpful at best, irrelevant at worst, in tracking the movement of the self toward conversion.[24] But if the conventional language of conversion was unable to achieve its desired intent, it was nonetheless crucial in allowing for Protestant pietists to construct themselves within modernist discourse.

If the Puritan narrators could at least lay claim to some ecclesiastical purpose for relating their conversion experiences, evangelical spiritual autobiographers had no such privilege. Even if the autobiographer belonged to a communion that demanded a similar relation, the spiritual autobiography was generally not produced for that purpose. The act of autobiography created a language of the self that intensified the paradoxes of evangelical discourse because in their autobiographies evangelicals continued to speak the orthodox language of Protestant pietism. Like the Puritans, evangelicals turned "inward" but also "outward," with their emphasis increasingly placed on the latter perspective. "Self-examination," wrote Charles G. Finney in words far removed from Shepard's prescription, "consists in looking at your lives, in considering your actions, in calling up the past, and learning its true character. Look back on your past history."[25] Conversion was not only the narrative apex from which the self could be objectified and constructed; it was the discursive medium through which evangelicals could cross "to and fro" between the orthodox and eternal soul and the modern temporal self.

Still, evangelical autobiographers continued to echo the pietistic language of humiliation. "I was less than nothing in my own sight," Freeborn Garrettson wrote, while others adopted even stronger language. "I longed for annihilation," wrote the Baptist missionary Ann Judson, "and if I could have destroyed the existence of my soul, with as much ease as that of my body, I should quickly have done it." In the morphology of evangelical con-version, true conversion was necessarily preceded by a period of "conviction" during which the convert was supposed to feel sensibly the angst of proper humiliation. "At length I gave way to despair, and had the worst apprehensions of punishment for my sins," wrote George W. Batchelder of his experience of conviction. "My sins increased, and appeared to rise like mountains before me. My soul was convulsed within me."[26]

Conviction was a narrative device used to set the stage for what was to follow, and evangelical autobiographers often used standard formulas to give expression to this preconversion despair. The Congregationalist minister Elam Potter repeated a familiar refrain when he lamented, "I often wished in the bitterness of my soul, that I had never been born"; and Asa Wild's declaration that as a young man he was "one of the greatest adepts in wickedness" echoed numerous other autobiographers who claimed, in Pauline metaphor, to be "chief of sinners." Others adopted more picturesque language. "My soul was weighed down with a burden of sin like a cart loaded with sheaves," wrote Baptist Hosea Smith; and even the eccentric Wild reported, "I felt my heart to be a *sink* of sin, a *cage* of uncleanness, a *fountain* of corruption."[27]

Such claims of sinfulness and great wickedness were obviously contrived in order to fit the conversion morphology, and so taxonomies of sins—such as Peter Cartwright's famous description that he was "a wild wicked boy . . . [who] delighted in horse-racing, card-playing, and dancing"—do indeed seem disingenuous and make the narrative appear to be "not so much composed as recited."[28] In some cases, even the autobiographers themselves recognized the artificial nature of this component. Hosea Smith still felt it necessary to depict his preconversion life as one of sin even though he was orphaned at an early age and a victim of extreme abuse as a child. Listing a traditional litany of sins such as lying, anger, and taking in vain the name of God, Smith paused at one point and queried, given the evil that he all too often had been the recipient of, whether his peccadilloes were "worth repenting for."[29] Smith's moment of candor was rare, however; few autobiographers seemed troubled by magnifying their childhood transgressions for the sake of the narrative expectation.

The problem is not that autobiographers used such conventions, but that their employment of them actually subverted their intentions. For every time the narrator lay claim to being "the chief of sinners," he or she expressed a hubris that disrupted the theological ideal. Typical were the contradictory observations of Ray Potter, who claimed no religious instruction as a child and lamented, "I have found myself to be one of the greatest sinners that ever the world bore up." Yet, wrote Potter,

> I cannot recollect the time when I did not look upon what is generally termed dishonesty with the utmost abhorrence. . . . One day, when about seven years old, as it was a fashionable thing with my play-mates, I thought I would use profane language, and not be so singular. But it seemed impossible. I uttered one or two oaths, when I became so panic-struck with the thought of taking the name of God in vain, that I abandoned it forever. . . . I never to my recollection inflicted a blow on one of my play-mates or companions in youth. And this not because I feared being vanquished, (for I reigned king among them in wrestling, on which I valued myself) but because my natural feelings revolted at the sight of suffering and distress.[30]

This self-proclaimed "greatest of sinners" could not abide dishonesty, refused to swear oaths, and could not bring himself to lift his hand against his fellows, even while a child. Indeed, the only sin that seems to be apparent in Potter's account of his conviction is his conceit in his exemplary behavior.

Pride, in fact, was the unescapable sin of all spiritual autobiographers, and they were powerless to excise it from their narratives. On the one hand, it came to be the predominant symbol for their preconversion life of sin; but, on the other hand, they had to struggle hard to keep it from infecting their postconversion narrative lives. Few were as pompous as Nathanael Emmons, who wrote that he "was never noted for falsehood, profaneness, Sabbath breaking, or a great fondness for vain company," and while still "quite young, . . . had many serious thoughts," but hubris affected the most conscientious of narratives.[31] In the hands of most autobiographers, even a pious youth such as Emmons described could become a target for preconversion denunciation. Ann Judson and Elam Potter both admitted being raised by pious parents and, in Potter's words, "kept back from outward immoralities." Potter even professed the covenant and was receiving communion by age nineteen, yet, he wrote, "I saw plainly that my heart was not right with God. . . . that in the solemn worship of God I had no delight." The Methodist minister Freeborn Garrettson recalled that as a child he had been taught "the Lord's prayer, creed, and ten commandments, together with the catechism of the church of England," and though restrained by his parents from "open sin," he cautioned his readers that these things did not truly represent him: "I was careless, and carnal, though what the world calls a moral youth."[32] As in Ray Potter's account, what was supposed to demonstrate humility negated its intention. Even when the self was supposed to be presented, by the conventions of the morphology, as utterly depraved, sinful, and in need of extinction, evangelical autobiographers found themselves unable to accomplish the task. Garrettson, Potter, and many others present themselves as exemplary Christians in spite of themselves—often before, and certainly after, their conversions. Clearly, the pietist morphology of conversion could not control the expression.

Such despair was necessary in the narrative, however, because it established the proper tension for the catharsis of conversion. "I now saw clearly," Theophilus Gates could write after his conversion, "that all the disappointments and afflictions I had experienced, were indispensably necessary to suppress my aspiring nature, humble my proud heart, and draw me away from the love of the world and its vanities." Similarly, Eleazar Sherman wrote, "As soon as I had given up all, I found peace, and the glory of God filled my soul."[33]

The ambivalence of self only glimpsed within the discourse of Puritanism—where the speaking self validated the experiencing self through language—was the critical problem for evangelical autobiographers because the problem of the "I" that Elias Smith, Abner Chase, and many others identified had become a more significant problem of American culture by the early nineteenth century. In religion, especially in Protestant pietism, the stress on personal experience and voluntary association were concepts that made sense only within a larger cultural matrix that valued the autonomy of the individual to decide or make choices. The life of grace itself became a matter of choice for such pietists, who, try as they might to discount the ability of the self to choose correctly, realized nonetheless that conversion too had become a matter of personal decision. "The conversion of a sinner consists in his obeying the truth," asserted Charles G. Finney in his famous lectures on revivalism. "It is therefore impossible it should take place without his agency, for it consists in *his* acting right. . . . What sinners do is to submit to the truth or resist it."[34]

In their conversion narratives and spiritual autobiographies, evangelical authors often commented upon the array of choices that confronted them, including, as implied in Finney's statement, the ability to accept or to reject grace and conversion. If grace was the free gift of God to the sinner, it was nevertheless incumbent upon the recipient to accept it volitionally. As Freeborn Garrettson expressed it: "the Lord met me powerfully with these words . . . 'I have come once more to offer you life and salvation, and it is the last time: chuse or refuse.'. . . I do believe if I had rejected this call, mercy would have been forever taken from me." The willfulness is even more apparent in the account of Joseph Thomas: "early in the morning . . . when I arose I stood in the yard looking up to heaven and determined before God that I would retire to a certain vale in the woods and if there was any pardon for my sins and redemption for my soul that there I would pray and wrestle until I would obtain [it]."[35]

As Thomas's account implies, physical movement became an important metaphor for conversion in evangelical narratives, made even more significant by the fact that the proliferation of popular denominations in the early nineteenth century actually allowed the author to wander from group to group in a type of religious quest that underscored his ability to "chuse or refuse." Prior to his conversion, Joshua Comstock claimed to have been successively a deist and then a Universalist, and George Batchelder experienced an evangelical conversion at the age of twenty but joined first with the Universalists before settling into the more appropriate Methodism. Harriet Livermore had an even more complex journey through various denominations. Born and baptized an Episcopalian, she was attracted to the Quakers but joined the Congregationalists and later the Freewill Baptists before finally associating with Elias Smith's Christian Connection—all before the age of fifteen![36] With Livermore and her mentor, Smith, many others, such as Abner Jones, Levi Hathaway, Eleazar Sherman, and Barton Stone expressed confusion and concern at the variety of religious choices that were presented to them, and each eventually forsook all denominational labels and referred to themselves simply as "Christians." Outside of the evangelical denominations, the new plurality of choices in religious affiliation led to personal confusion and, in the case of Joseph Smith Jr., to the establishment of a competing denomination. Yet even the converts to Smith's new "Church of Christ" exemplified the tendency to have sampled a number of denominations before joining with the Latter-day Saints.[37] For seekers such as Batchelder, Livermore, and Joseph Smith, making the correct choice was crucial because of the eternal consequences it represented for them; but in another sense, it was crucial because it marked, in many ways, the beginning of a stable center from which other contingencies and life choices could be evaluated and weighed. It marked, in other words, the deliberate decision to achieve full selfhood, and so was particularly appealing to adolescents or young adults who stood at the threshold of social maturity.[38]

In justifying themselves through the production of a spiritual autobiography, evangelical authors justified the rise of a new literary genre in America that reflected a new age, a new spirit. If conversion was theologically egalitarian—at least in theory—because it presented to and demanded of all the choice of grace or damnation, spiritual autobiography and conversion narratives were similarly the first "democratic" forms of literature because they legitimated the narrative self they produced on the basis of their use of the discourse of conversion.

There was a clear connection between the political rhetoric of democracy and the rise of new religious forms in antebellum America. The years between 1780 and 1830 marked a "transitional period" during which the language of popular political sovereignty was translated into a religious idiom by evangelical groups such as the Baptists and Methodists, black evangelical churches such as the African Methodist Episcopal Church, the transdenominational Christian restorationist movements of Barton Stone, Elias Smith, and even Joseph Smith's Latter-day Saints. "Intent on bringing evangelical conversion to the mass of ordinary Americans," Nathan O. Hatch noted, "[evangelical leaders] could rarely divorce that message from contagious new democratic vocabularies and impulses that swept through American popular cultures." In similar fashion, Gary L. Ebersole has described a "democratization . . . of the ability to interpret texts" that established a "new reading covenant" in the antebellum years.[39] Far from being merely imitative texts, evangelical spiritual autobiographies were part of new vernacular and modernist literature that reflected the language of popular democracy, but they were not without the tension that accompanies any new discursive formation.

Faced with the need to speak about conversion by justifying themselves, many evangelical spiritual autobiographers struggled with the discursive power that had been given them. "Many consider it impracticable and beneath their dignity to publish the memoirs of their life themselves, while living," wrote Ray Potter. "But why so? I think it *sometimes* expedient, and a duty. Great and good men have frequently done it. It may be argued that though *great* men have seen fit to do it, and in so doing they have benefitted mankind, yet that is no reason that an obscure individual, like myself, should undertake it. To which I answer; that although I may not be a great man, yet I am very sure that God has done *great things* for me; and most certainly it should be the design of all Christians, not to endeavour to shew *themselves* great, but to magnify the name of the Lord God."[40]

The rhetorical strategies of Potter typify the contradictions and tensions that faced other evangelical authors, who, like Potter, struggled with the issue of justifying the transformation of their lives into narrative. Potter's literary confrontation with greatness and obscurity should not be read as a false modesty but as a sincere struggle with the self within a new, and more democratic, context. If the discourse of conversion vindicated the production of an autobiographical text, it also extended the authority of the experiencing self to anyone who could write—or relate—an experience of conversion. "Why write the biography of a 'common man' when so many of famous men are available?" queried the unnamed compiler of John Oliphant's memoirs. Why indeed? The answer was simple: "The most of the Biographies, which are making their appearance, recite the actions of those who have moved in peculiar circles, or been employed in peculiar works of benevolence. . . . But alas, too many, who are embarked in the ordinary business of life, do not consider the lives of these distinguished persons as affording examples for them to imitate. With respect to what is contained in this volume, it exhibits religion as it has existed, and as it may still exist, among persons in the common walks of life."[41]

The primary significance of Oliphant's autobiography lay in the very fact that its subject was one engaged "in the ordinary business of life" as presumably readers of the work would be, and it was thus able to speak to them in a way that more elite works of literature could not. Further, in speaking of themselves by narrating their conversion experience, evangelicals such as Potter and Oliphant opened the way for the creation of a new vernacular literature that allowed otherwise "undistinguished" persons to create themselves as objects of discourse. "In looking through the libraries of our country," wrote the Methodist George Henry in 1846, "we find the histories of many of the best and most eminent men . . . and find there also the story of those, whose devious course through life was marked only by the vilest acts and the multiplied evils they inflicted on their race." While the "former of these characters are so far above, and the latter so far beneath the walk of the great mass of community," Henry commented, "perhaps it is not so interesting or profitable to pursue the history of their lives, as to trace the life of one whose course has been between these two extremes." In offering himself as an exemplar of the democratic middle, Henry participated in evangelical redemption of the self, not so much through religious experience as through linguistic presentation.[42]

Despite their problems of expression, despite their reversal of goals, despite their inability to accomplish what they set out to do, evangelical spiritual autobiographers contributed to a popular discourse that allowed for the emergence of the modern self within American Protestantism. If they were, like Elias Smith and Abner Chase, ultimately unable to overcome the problem of the "I," they were able, nevertheless, to offer an innovative linguistic form through which the self might be appropriately expressed and controlled. The conversion contained within their texts was one that turned the self from spiritual renegade to evangelical exemplar. In narratively creating themselves, evangelicals converted themselves, and from auditors of the word they were transformed into authors of the word.

CHAPTER FOUR

THE LANGUAGE
OF EXPERIENCE

*I had never heard a person relate a Christian experience; and my
experience came so different from my expectation, that I thought I
must go through something more, to be born again. At length a young
man, who I believed was born again, told me his religious change.
This was instrumental of my receiving evidence that I had been born
of the Holy Spirit: for "as face answers to face in water" so did his
Christian experience answer unto mine.*

—James Hooper, 1834

By their expectation that converts could give autobiographical voice to their conversions, pietists assigned a
powerful and dynamic role to language. As indicated by
the Baptist autobiographer James Hooper, it was through
words, through language, through discourse, that conversion itself could be engendered, realized, and proclaimed.
The "Word" was a powerful metaphor in evangelical life
that not only referred to the biblical text, but was synony-
mous with the redemptive and converting power of God.
"The scripture is full of instances, sufficient to convince
us," argued Jonathan Edwards, "that if the word of God
will not awaken and convert sinners, nothing will." In
similar fashion, Barton Stone asserted, "The word of God

is the seed of regeneration . . . the word of truth is the means of enlightening, quickening, regenerating and sanctifying the soul. . . . His word is his power to salvation." To be sure, neither Edwards nor Stone envisioned the word to act in the absence of faith or contrary to proper "application" in the life of the individual; yet, as Stone explained further, "faith does not depend on any disposition, whether holy or unholy; but on the strength of the testimony. No Christian will deny that there is sufficient evidence in the word to produce faith. . . . [Faith] *is admitting testimony upon the authority of the testifier. Or it is simply believing the testimony of God.*"[1] In the language of evangelical pietism, nothing but the word could "pierce the heart" of the sinner; and in offering one's own testimony through oral relation or spiritual autobiography, nothing but the word could validate the experience of conversion.

The terminology was not accidental; as the perceived seat of the affections in premodern psychology, the "heart" was the organ that pietists wanted most to touch through their words, and pietist denunciations of rhetorical eloquence do not imply a rejection of language to operate principally through the emotions. "Art and eloquence," Debora K. Shuger points out, may have been "only hindrances, clogging up the transfer of divine energy with sensual distractions," but Protestant rhetors nevertheless held that "[p]assionate language mirrors the inward ardor of the speaker." Thus, the so-called "plain style" of preaching championed by pietist ministers did not assume, as its title might imply, an unimaginative correspondence between thing and word, but rather a new investment in a "Christian rhetoric" that "operates according to sacramental rather than dialectical modes," according to Shuger, because "[i]t incarnates the spiritual and elicits the affective/intuitive response that can spring from visible sign to invisible reality."[2] Words might obscure and confuse at times, but they were, for the pietist, also able to convict and convert because they carried a potency in relation to the things they named far more than any image could.

In their dependence upon the word to form the essential center of the Christian life, evangelicals such as Edwards and Stone affirmed their Protestant heritage by reconstructing Christianity in the image of the text rather than the text of an image. "The image was not peripheral to medieval Christianity," Margaret Aston reminds us; "It was a central means for the individual to establish contact with God."[3] Therefore, when the reformers and revolutionaries challenged the institutions of late medieval culture, they were not only seeking alternative foundations for their authority (for example, in scripture) but also offering a diametrically opposed means of constructing social reality. Not only did this involve the iconoclasm that was directed against statuary and other images by many Protestants, but also an iconoclasm against traditional ways of perceiving religious truth. Signs and sacraments, John Calvin had argued, might be allowed in condescension to the deficiencies of human nature, but the Word of God was best mediated only through words, and so the Protestant often rejected all forms of knowing beyond that offered by words and texts. The result of this linguistic dependence was that words themselves began to carry sacramental value.

The English Protestantism from which Puritanism would arise was even more severe in its rejection of the image for the word. The "covenant theology" of Puritanism, which read even the process of redemption itself in the form of a textual contract, was informed by a long-standing iconoclastic heritage in England that was traceable at least to the fourteenth-century reform movement known as Lollardy. The Lollards had been more radical than the later Continental Reformation would be in their displacement of visual in favor of the verbal, and it was from this tradition, not from classical Calvinism, that English Puritans drew many of their misgivings concerning imagery and nonverbal expressions. When the Reformation spread to England, rigid iconoclasm was an instinctive response for a people already accustomed to viewing art and symbolism with grave suspicion, and who saw in the late-medieval Catholic sense of aesthetic a further sign of the accretions of the Roman Church upon the primitive Christian reliance on the "good news." In a similar way, the elaborate liturgical forms surrounding the sacraments demonstrated the gap, as perceived by the Puritans, between the simplicity of the gospel and the pretensions of the Catholic faith. The visual, whether in art or sacrament, always ran the risk of obscuring the very thing it was supposed to proclaim—the "Word." According to John Dillenberger, "While the continentals interpreted the Word as the light that shines into our darkness without dispelling all the shadows, the English saw the Word as the light whose clarity takes all shadows away. . . . [L]anguage was a clarifying act, enabling one to say, 'Now I see.'"[4]

Preaching was the preferred means of such clarification for pietists. Making the effort to attend and hear sermons, lectures, and "prophesyings" by Puritan ministers was usually a sure sign of one's Puritan sympathies in both

Old and New England. "[T]he mark of the lay Puritan," noted Paul S. Seaver, "was his demand for constant preaching," and attendance at the Elizabethan lectureships dominated by Puritan ministers became "a public action that revealed the inward character of the saint." No such mechanisms were necessary in the godly commonwealths of New England, where Puritan ministers controlled the pulpits and mandatory church attendance ensured them of an audience. Hearing the Word was an inescapable fact of life in Puritan New England, and according to Harry S. Stout's study of the Puritan sermon in America, "The average weekly churchgoer in New England listened to something like seven thousand sermons in a lifetime, totaling somewhere around fifteen thousand hours of concentrated listening."[5] Puritanism, and later evangelicalism, embodied the Pauline proclamation that "faith cometh by hearing, and hearing by the word of God" (Rom. 10:17b, KJV).

In the Puritan terminology, sermons were the "means" of grace, the principal way in which God began the process of conversion. "It was through a sermon that nine out of ten of the elect caught the first hints of their vocation," wrote Perry Miller, "and by continued listening to good preaching they made their calling sure." Although other sources might offer similar benefits, none displaced the sermon as the primary means to grace. "O, therefore, if ever you would have the spirit dispensed to you," Thomas Shepard implored his congregation from the pulpit of First Church in Cambridge, "wait here upon the ministry of the gospel for it; neglect not private helps, books and meditations, etc., but know, if ever you have it dispensed, here it is chiefly to be had, buy at this shop."[6]

Desire to hear the Word properly preached often propelled the Puritan on a peripatetic quest in search of the elusive commodity of grace that was at once both figurative and literal. Shepard's collection of oral relations offers some examples of such auditory crusades. Edward Collins recounted his search for "further means and helps" through Wethersfield, Colne, London, and Dedham in Old England before his migration to New England, which he presented as little more than a continuation of his literal pilgrimage toward the Word. The relation of "Goodman With" (Nicholas Wyeth) was even more illustrative of the Puritan pursuit "to go and hear":

I went out to hear the word . . . And going to hear one Mr. Salby [Robert Selby] I did much affect his ministry and did somewhat profit by it. . . . And the Lord kept me and encouraged me hereby much still to go and hear other good men. And every Sabbath day I went four miles to hear him [for] about a year. . . . And I took every opportunity I could and could get liberty of my master to go out to hear. . . . And so I lived twelve years and [the] Lord brought Mr. Burrows [Jeremiah Burroughes] some sixteen miles off and I was then able-bodied then and went often to hear him. . . . And I saw I was in my natural condition yet I went out to hear and went twenty miles off to Mr. Rogers . . . but though I did hear much yet I could not see my heart was brought so near as I did desire, for I had been very careless in remembering what I heard and for sixteen years went on so in old England. Hence I came to New England.[7]

The cadences of Wyeth's account in his repeatedly going "out to hear" certainly convey the importance of the oral culture that infused Puritanism and made the spoken word, through the sermon, a symbol for the entire movement. Darrett Rutman's wry observation that Puritanism was "a gift imparted by the preachers . . . to the laymen who heard them preaching" seems to be only a mild exaggeration of the circumstances that drove Collins, Wyeth, and countless others to seek "further means and helps" across the landscapes of both Old and New England.[8]

The power to speak—to preach—was, as Rutman's comment suggests, the power to control. The sermon lay at the heart of Puritan discourse, and through the medium of the sermon Puritan ministers participated in and sustained this discourse by sanctioning the "knowledge" of conversion. In almost every relation recorded by Shepard, the narrator noted the Puritan preacher who was responsible, in part, for his or her discernment of conversion. But this control was not absolute; indeed, it was directly proportional to the ability—or willingness—of the preacher to assume the language of the discourse. Although the laity may have "received" their Puritanism from the hands of the ministers, it was their willingness to "hear" that sanctioned the authority of the ministers. Wyeth's determined ventures to travel where he could "hear" denotes his strong rejection of those ministers who did not conform their speaking to the discourse of Puritan pietism. His willingness to participate in this alternate discursive reality indicated the power of autonomy that such discursive choices made possible, but it also demonstrated the necessary connection between Protestantism and the linguistic revolution of the early modern West. Divorced, at least theoretically, from sacramental and liturgical activity that required seeing, touching, smelling, and tasting, the fortunes of Protestantism depended on its almost total investment in speaking and hearing, or, alternately, in writing and reading.

The sermon, of course, became the distinguishing feature in the evangelical conception of the role of the minister, and it was the principal method of evangelism in both local congregational meetings and mass revivals. The "great end" of the office of the minister according to Charles G. Finney, was "the salvation of souls"; and Finney charged that this was best accomplished through the minister's use of properly affective language. "Truth, when brought to bear upon the mind," he wrote, "is in itself calculated to produce corresponding feelings. The minister must know what feelings he wishes to produce, and how to bring such truth to bear as is calculated to produce these feelings."[9] Despite this continued dependence on affective preaching to convert individuals, few antebellum spiritual autobiographers actually claimed to have experienced conversion as the direct result of a sermon. Jarena Lee wrote that her "soul was gloriously converted to God, under preaching, at the very outset of the sermon," and Peter Cartwright recorded his conversion experience as having occurred during the altar call that followed the sermon at a camp meeting, but these were exceptions to an otherwise standard denial that conversion had been brought about through a sermon. "Evangelical, powerful, reformation preaching, I never heard till after I was converted," claimed Harriet Livermore, echoing a typical refrain that placed most autobiographers apart from any traditional sermonic setting at the moment of their conversions.[10] This unwillingness on the part of the evangelical authors to acknowledge the influence of preaching or the setting of a worship service will be examined later; for now, it is sufficient only to understand that such disclaimers were more of a rhetorical device than a statement of fact. The evangelical autobiographers lived during an age saturated with sermons, and, despite their proclaimed ignorance, their narratives offer a few glimpses of the influence of sermons and ministers in their lives. Eleazer Sherman sounded like a Puritan in recounting his quest to go and hear various ministers preach, and Ann Judson made frequent reference to her attendance at sermons. John Hudson and Freeborn Garrettson both reported their convictions began under preaching, and even when attendance at a sermon was for a decidedly impious reason, the sermon possessed the power to convict and convert. James Champlin divulged that his conviction came about as the result of his presence at a Baptist meeting. He had gone intending to ridicule the preacher but was instead motivated by the words of the sermon to seek conversion. According to the evangelical understanding, the Word that lay behind the words of the sermon always assumed a universal validity and thus could always produce the intended result. "[W]hen I heard preaching, even by strange ministers," wrote Henry Holcombe, "it seemed to be intentionally accommodated to my case."[11]

By the early years of the nineteenth century, changes in printing processes (which brought down the cost of books and allowed for mass publication) and increased access to education (which brought rising literacy rates) made devotional literature more accessible to the wider population than it had ever been before.[12] Pious reading had been a part of Protestant devotional life since the beginning of the Reformation. As Thomas Shepard noted, "private helps, books and meditations" could be acceptable alternatives to hearing sermons when occasion demanded. The most important devotional text, of course, was the Bible, but Protestants were not only a People of the Book, they were a people of books, and for their personal devotions a variety of devotional manuals, printed sermons, and pious tracts often filled more immediate needs. Like the sermons, such devotional reading was understood as discursively creative as well as intellectually stimulating. In fact, argues Charles E. Hambrick-Stowe in his study of Puritan devotional literature, "The reading and study of religious texts, though an intellectual activity, did not primarily or finally have an intellectual end. The exercise of the rational faculty opened the way to a changed heart."[13] The same elements that gave the sermon its power informed the act of devotional reading as well: words elucidated by the Word that had as their goal the discernment of conversion. Such reading was thus at once a pious and a performative activity.

The antebellum spiritual autobiographies present their own evidence that reading pious literature was often closely linked with obtaining a conversion experience. Like numerous evangelicals, Elam Potter sought solace in the Bible, although during his period of conviction he felt that "I was the mark to which all it's woes were pointed, and I saw not one promise for me." Other texts, however, were often just as influential if not more so for some authors. Potter mentioned his reading of martyrologies, and Freeborn Garrettson reported that during his conviction, "I now procured a collection of the best religious books that I could," adding, "I frequently read, prayed, and wept till after midnight." Likewise, Ann Judson recalled that she made extensive use of "religious magazines" and that during her period of conviction she "spent [her] days in reading and crying for mercy" for some two to three weeks. Echoing Elam Potter's despair at reading the Bible, Devereux Jarratt claimed that he could not find any relief by reading books or even in hearing sermons, although when his conversion occurred he reported that there was "a good *book* in my hand."[14] Oral testimony continued to be significant for some. In recounting his conversion experience, for example, Ephraim Stinchfield disclosed that he "read all the books I could find, on religious experience," but that he also "endeavored to get all the instruction in my power, from persons of experience, as to what they passed through, and how they found relief." Of course, such devotional texts or oral accounts would have been permeated with biblical language, and while a surprisingly small number of autobiographers actually quoted influential biblical texts, many autobiographers made little distinction between the actual text of the Bible and its duplication in a devotional work or devout testimony. "One day fatigued with mowing I came in at noon and went into a room by myself to read in Marshall's book," wrote James Hooper, "and as I read I came to these words, 'Behold, now is the accepted time; behold, now is the day of salvation' [2 Cor. 6:2]. When I read these words, as quick as a flash of lightning from heaven, I saw God's law was holy, just, and good.—I also saw my own heart."[15] Although the otherwise unidentified "Marshall's book" provided the immediate text, the actual text—the Word that empowered the word—was biblical, though not explicitly distinguished as such by Hooper.

The world of the evangelical was thus a world of words that were spoken, heard, printed, and read; and both pious reading and pious hearing served as catalysts for personal experience. The actions of writing, reading, composing, speaking, and hearing were all regarded by evangelicals as integral components within the process of conversion. To term these activities as constituting the elements of the discourse of conversion simply recognizes, by use of a different terminology, what evangelicals had already discovered. The Protestant confidence in the ability of words to make sacramentally real that which was otherwise elusively transcendent made the language of conversion a significant part of the conversion process. Assigning sacramental value to the act of language—even to the words themselves—meant that speaking and hearing, writing and reading, had the potency to become for the evangelical religious actions.

Despite its potency, however, the language of conversion has always presented great interpretive problems, especially for modern readers who find the orthodox and highly conventional style stilted and strained. Unlike the confidence that Protestants professed in the ability of the word to clarify and elucidate, the customary language of evangelical conversion has generally been regarded as an obscuring rather than a clarifying mechanism. Common words and phrases that often echoed, even if they did not directly quote, the biblical text, coupled with the pattern of the conversion genre that presumed the denouement from the very beginning, generated a conventional rhetorical pattern that seems to eclipse the autonomous self that forms the nucleus of any authentic autobiographical expression. The spiritual autobiographer was thus seemingly caught in a dilemma created by her use of the formulaic language of conversion. There can be little doubt that it is the use of such language that has led many contemporary interpreters to suggest that the formula employed served only as a didactic or mnemonic stratagem that provided potential converts with the proper pattern for their own conversions.[16]

While it cannot be denied that evangelicals viewed their narratives as teaching devices, one might question the simplicity of this answer given the status of language in the Protestant mind. Certainly many evangelical autobiographers considered their texts to have a prescriptive utility. Freeborn Garrettson wrote that he had "an ardent desire to be useful," and so "advise[d] all those into whose hands this short diary may fall, to read it with earnest prayer; then peradventure it will have its desired effect on their hearts. In this account I did by no means intend to gratify the curiosity, or to tickle the ears of those who live in pleasure. . . . I aim . . . to be instrumental in bringing precious souls to the Lord Jesus Christ." Likewise, George Henry recorded his prayerful hope "that in the hand of God [my narrative] may be instrumental in directing the mind of the reader, while he is traveling through this 'vale of tears,' and enduring the trials and disappointments of life, to the great Fountain of happiness here and of eternal life beyond the grave."[17] But the necessity of constantly reiterating the same form in the same words in order to encourage conversion on the part of the reader seems needlessly redundant. As Virginia Lieson Brereton points out, "Most prospective converts were drenched in the language of conversion from birth."[18] Why then would the spiritual autobiographers have felt a need to repeat a formula with which most of their readers would have been intimately familiar? Interpreting the language of these texts primarily as a teaching device ignores the complex roles that such rhetoric could assume within the larger discursive formation.

Placing the language of conversion within the discursive understanding of Protestant pietism suggests that more was involved than mere repetition. Within the discursive formations of Protestant evangelicalism, the rhetoric of conversion served two interrelated purposes: To constitute the experience of conversion itself and also to form the discursive community that sanctioned it.

Given the alchemical linkage between word and object in the Protestant mind, it may be argued that the conversion narratives actually *performed* the action of conversion. Each individual conversion was a reflection of God's (already determined) redemptive activity, yet each reflection was imperfect not because conversion was somehow incomplete or defective but because it involved that autonomous entity, the self. Yet, in the same way that the action of autobiography created the self of the author, so the language of conversion made the experience of conversion a reality because it placed it within the discursive domain of the author. As illustrated by the quotation from James Hooper's autobiography that begins this chapter, words had the power to formulate, to structure, and to bring about the recognition of conversion. He had never heard a conversion experience related before, so Hooper informs his reader. It was only in confronting such a narration that his own experience became fully manifested; and this act of hearing "was instrumental of my receiving evidence that I had been born of the Holy Spirit." For many evangelicals, conversion was "incomplete"—unrecognized—until it was formed and structured through the rhetoric of conversion discourse; the "experience" of conversion was consummated only by their ability to speak the language of conversion.

With James Hooper, many evangelical autobiographers claimed never to have heard the relation of a conversion experience before they themselves were converted. What evangelicals did acknowledge, however, was the performative function of conversion language; that is, the ability of such language not only to present models of conversion, but also to *create* the reality of the event through the act of language itself. When the prospective church member in colonial New England offered her oral relation of conversion, or when a later evangelical penned his spiritual autobiography, each engaged in the action of not only describing and representing the experience but also narratively creating it. Just as Hooper's hearing a young man relate his experience provided him with the "evidence" that his conversion had indeed occurred, evangelical autobiographers often ascribed their conversions to corresponding situations. "[A] few weeks after I was baptized," wrote Ray Potter, "I heard an experience related, and a Christian describing the work of grace on the heart ... and felt assured that I had experienced it myself."[19] Conversion discourse was a linguistic strategy that evangelicals exploited in order to do far more than merely describe experience or imitate antecedent paradigms. As the experiences of Hooper and Potter demonstrated, conversion was a creative linguistic process that reflected the logical end of the Protestant concept of the power of the word to perform—by giving shape and form to individual experience—what it also described. Put another way, conversion was, like the self, a creation of the autobiographical act.[20]

Many evangelical autobiographers claimed to have realized and fully appropriated their own conversions only after the fact, when they were confronted with some further narrative presentation (either oral or written). For James Hooper and Ray Potter this was accomplished through hearing the account of other converts, but this retrospective experience could take other forms as well. Abner Jones, for example, simply recalled a biblical verse that eased his doubt and validated his experience on the day following his initial conversion experience.[21] Since all spiritual autobiographies were written from a postconversion position, such retrospection was an absolute necessity for properly understanding the process of conversion. It provided the proper perspective from which both the author's pre- and postconversion life could be viewed as a coherent whole and assigned meaning within an evangelical framework. "I then looked back on my past life," wrote the restorationist autobiographer Eleazer Sherman, "and saw from a child I had refused that Spirit which was sent to reprove the world of sin, of righteousness and of judgment."[22]

The ability of conversionist discourse to create personal meaning was especially crucial because its referent—the personal experience of the convert—was generally considered to be beyond expression. Conversion was ultimately an ineffable experience, available only subjectively to the convert and beyond the power of language to objectify. This problem was stated often by evangelical autobiographers. Abner Chase commented that his conversion took place "in a manner which I cannot describe"; and Theophilus Gates wrote that during his experience of conversion he "had such a sight of the wisdom of God in the plan of salvation; and felt such a love in my heart towards him and all mankind as can never be expressed by words, nor any one have any idea of, unless they have experienced it themselves."[23] One may read such disclaimers as empty platitudes of piety, but they reflected the struggles that spiritual autobiographers faced when confronted with the problem of describing an experience beyond description. By giving form and structure to such individual experiences, the rhetoric of conversion provided converts with a pattern through which their ineffable experience could not only be articulated, but also legitimated by the community. The discourse created the reality of the conversion, and thus the choice of language on the part of the convert was deliberate and allowed spiritual autobiographers to integrate "a shared religious language into the idiosyncratic details of their own life histories and situations."[24]

Whatever the nature of the subjective experience it claims to name, conversion language represents a particular way of speaking (or writing). Learning to speak the language of conversion was in itself part of the conversion process since the rhetoric of conversion engaged both the speaker and the listener in a dialogic transformation of narrative reality. The principal task of the speaker was not to offer merely a model to be imitated but to construct a narrative world into which the listener could be drawn. Acceptance or denial of conversion (on the part of the auditor) would then be predicated upon the internal logic of this narrative reality and the willingness of the listener to place himself or herself within this narrative frame of reference. The ability to identify with this narrative reality marked the degree to which the auditor internalized the rhetorical demands of the language of conversion. In the words of Susan Harding, the language of conversion is both "an *argument* about the transformation of self that lost souls must undergo, and a *method* of bringing about that change in those who

listen to it." Conversion testimony is thus "not just a monologue that constitutes its speaker as a culturally specific person; it is also a dialogue that
reconstitutes its listeners."[25]

Thus the evangelistic intentions expressed by Freeborn Garrettson and
George Henry must be read as more than pious sentiment and more than
offering a mnemonic device or instructive paradigm. Their design was to
transform both author and reader through the interactive character of the
narrative itself. Henry Holcombe depicted this dialogic process when he
imagined the unconverted reader beseeching the author "if you know that
[evangelical Christianity] is a system of vital and energetic truth, strongly
tending to holiness and happiness, explain to us as familiarly as possible, how
you came by this invaluable knowledge."[26] Conversion rhetoric was intended to produce, not just recount, conversion. Evangelical autobiographers demanded that "sinners" confront the experience of grace and salvation *within the context of narrative:* only this could give one power to "see
and feel" one's "undone" state; and only this could provide the means for
one to "embrace Christ by faith," according to the typical terminology
employed by Abner Chase.[27]

There thus existed a contract between the reader and the author and, by
extension, to the larger evangelical community as a whole. According to
Stanley Fish's analysis of the role of the community in instituting discursive relationships, formal and meaningful patterns do not exist objectively
within the discourse awaiting discovery but are, in Fish's words, "themselves
constituted by an interpretive act." Although it is the individual who brings
to bear the "interpretive act" on the text or language, he does not operate
in a vacuum void of predetermined meaning, because such interpretive acts
"proceed not from him but from the interpretive community of which he
is a member; they are, in effect, community property, and insofar as they at
once enable and limit the operations of his consciousness, he is too." "Indeed," Fish concludes, "it is interpretive communities, rather than either
the text or the reader, that produce meanings and are responsible for the
emergence of formal features."[28]

Conversion narratives assumed a powerful role within pietist communities. Since Puritans and many later evangelicals required public testimonies as a means to judge and validate the appropriateness of one's experience, such public performance obviously served as a powerful social tool in

providing an expected pattern of which converts would have been aware and would have used—perhaps subconsciously—in formulating their own testimonies despite their protests to the contrary. But even in the demanding atmosphere of the churches of colonial New England such a requirement of conformity to community standards seems not to have been too rigidly enforced. Many of the oral relations recorded by Thomas Shepard, for example, were vague and indeterminate, containing no real description of anything that might be labeled a conversion experience. Hannah Brewer, for example, reported of her despair over breaking the Sabbath and taking the Lord's name in vain, "but could apply nothing," meaning that the models of conversion so faithfully presented from the pulpit by Shepard carried no resonance with her own experiences. A Mrs. Greene delivered a similarly short and inconclusive testimony, but Shepard noted without further explanation that "[t]estimonies carried it," implying that Mrs. Greene was extended church membership despite her own inability to relate an experience that conformed to the conventional rhetorical expectations.[29] In the evangelical texts, the Baptist Ray Potter recorded a similar example of an individual inability to speak that was nonetheless sanctioned by the community. Only seventeen at the time, Potter found himself too frightened to speak when he stood before the congregation to relate his experience, and was able only to respond meekly to some questions put to him by the minister. Nevertheless, his relation was judged worthy by the congregation and he was welcomed into its fellowship. Such inarticulateness and failures of expression indicated the role of the discursive community to "underwrite," in the words of Baird Tipson, the experience of the individual, and demonstrated that the language of conversion belonged not to the individual but to the discursive community.[30]

This does not mean, however, that converts were tied to an inflexible morphology of conversion that determined the form of their experience. Fragmentary and unsatisfying relations such as those of Greene and Potter implied that, despite the approbation of the community, the narrators were often actually unable to harmonize their own experiences in any significant way to the conversion paradigm, presenting yet again the dichotomy between mythic ideal and historical reality that haunted spiritual autobiography. If the language seems stilted and unimaginative to contemporary readers, this is due to the discursive tasks that the language performed in constituting convert, conversion, and community. These constitutive responsibilities dominated the referential duties of the texts and thus must be understood as crucial components of the larger discursive goals. Evangelicals intended the language of conversion to be purposefully constructive of both conversion and convert (as both author and audience). The "ritual" cadences of evangelical conversionism achieved their power only within a particular community that implicitly lent its sanction to the "text" of conversion that the individual author appropriated as he or she (as a character) moved through the narrative landscape which they created.

CHAPTER FIVE

THE LANGUAGE OF
THE SACRED

*The "Journey of Life" with me commenced in the town of Hampton,
state of New-Hampshire. . . . Sept. 3d, 1818—was a very memorable
period of my life. Upon that auspicious day, the inestimable prize of
salvation, was vouchsafed to me. . . . The time, or the place, will
never be erased from my memory.*

—*Nancy Towle, 1833*

The intent of the language of conversion within the evangelical community was to represent, model, and effect
personal transformation. In creating themselves through
the process of autobiography, and in constituting the experience of conversion by their reliance on the capacity of
the word to create what it also represented, evangelicals
invested the language of conversion with transformative
potency. Conversion took place not only within their lives
but within their texts (both oral and written). In each recounting or with each rereading, the conversion of the
author as character was continually replicated, and the
auditor or reader of the text would likewise be challenged
to "convert" by adopting the language as his or her own
and thus affirm it as an acceptable expression of a common
discursive reality.

These performative and transformative expectations of conversion language were functions of the language act itself, which embodied a strong ritual structure. In describing her conversion as a "journey" through time and space—or, to be more precise, *toward* a particular time and *to* a particular place—Nancy Towle gave narrative expression to this ritual structure. If language could create the conversion event, it did so through the manipulation of linguistic signs that depicted the narrative movement of the autobiographer through space and time, reconciling, in the process, the contradictions raised by the activity of autobiography itself. The language of conversion not only allowed the evangelicals to speak of the self, it ritualized—and thus resolved—the various dichotomies that threatened the emergence of the self into Protestant orthodoxy. Like the autobiographical narrative itself, which mediated between the historical self and the mythic self, the narrative configuration of time and space in the evangelical autobiographies was a discursive trope that attempted to conciliate certain dialectic or contradictory concepts between the ideology and practical realization of conversion. Ultimately, the metaphors of time and space in the narratives provided the ritual matrix through which the linguistic transformation of conversion could take place.

Ritual, according to one classical argument, always takes shape in response to conditions that have the potential to cause significant social disruptions. When discrepancies or uncertainties arise that threaten to dissolve social bonds, societies often generate some form of symbolic activity that provides a way to channel these disorders into socially constructive, rather than destructive, ends.[1] While most such ritualization often takes the shape of "outward" or "embodied" behaviors, it can also occur, especially in modern societies, in the form of linguistic activities that can similarly enable individuals and societies to resolve such threatening disjunctions. Through the adoption and utilization of a "canonical language," Peter G. Stromberg asserts, modern individuals and societies can "go beyond the boundaries of the everyday, the predictable, the understandable" and can "establish certainty precisely where life seems least certain." Stromberg's study of contemporary evangelical conversion narratives leads him to argue that "[i]n the *ritual of the conversion narrative* in our own society believers seek to control the uncertain through using canonical language to formulate purposes that might otherwise take shape as mysterious and discomforting disturbances of communication."[2] This ritual operation of conversion language is not only a contemporary phenomenon. For a tradition so thoroughly imbued with the idea of the effectiveness of the Word to bring about significant personal change, antebellum evangelicalism depended wholly upon the language of conversion to provide the means by which the autonomous self could be meaningfully communicated or "spoken of." The spiritual autobiographies and conversion narratives of the antebellum evangelicals provided the discursive and ritual site from which, and *through* which, this transformation could be accomplished.

Evangelical autobiographers recognized this crucial link between language and experience and often commented on the ability of conversion rhetoric to validate and confirm their "prior" experiences. A comment by Ray Potter used in the previous chapter deserves to be quoted in full here: "When, . . . a few weeks after I was baptized, I heard an experience related, and a Christian describing the work of grace on the heart, my mind in a moment was carried back to the time and place where I experienced the *same* exercises, and then I knew what was meant by a religious experience, or a change of heart, and felt assured that I had experienced it myself."[3]

In being "carried back to the time and place" where he had experienced his conversion, Potter not only illustrated the constitutive function of conversion discourse but also echoed more generally Nancy Towle's association of conversion with specific spatial and temporal elements. Such concerns may be dismissed as either the simple presentation of historical or autobiographical "facts" or as concessions to the expected pattern, but their omnipresence in the narratives suggests their intrinsic importance as intentional and meaningful components in the discursive form of evangelical conversion. Numerous evangelical spiritual autobiographers followed Towle and Potter in emphasizing the time and place of their conversions; and in the narrative movement of the self through space and time, these autobiographers created the ritual structure of conversion.

Temporal and spatial location are significant components in any ritual activity. Rituals always occur within "sacred time," a "time" actually outside of temporality itself. Similarly, rituals occur within a "sacred space" that is "qualitatively different" from the territory around it because it reveals "an absolute fixed point" from which all else can be oriented.[4] For evangelicals, conversion represented an extension of the creative and regenerative activities of God that had occurred outside of historical time—either with the immutable decree of God before the creation of the world or in the "eternal" moment of the crucifixion when the process of human redemption had been ultimately completed—and its manifestation in the life of the individual shared in some way this transhistorical character. "I think I then saw, as clearly as I ever have in my life," wrote Charles G. Finney about his preconversion moment of truth, "the reality and fulness [*sic*] of the atonement of Christ. I saw that his work was a finished work. . . . Gospel salvation seemed to me to be an offer of something to be accepted; and that it was full and complete."[5] In more striking language, the Presbyterian minister Calvin Colton, attempting to explain conversion to his British readers, offered that "conversion, strictly speaking, considered as the turning of the heart, the act or suffering of regeneration, is not only sudden, but instantaneous—[so] that we cannot reckon a passage of time in the sinner's being born again . . . the new birth cannot occupy time."[6] On the other hand, American evangelicals were convinced, as perhaps no previous Christian tradition had been, that conversion occurred within a specific and identifiable moment of time. Nancy Towle, along with many other evangelicals, could cite the exact place and time; others, like Potter, at least underscored the significance of the time of their conversions, even if they did not note specifics. Like the self, conversion existed as both a mythic and a historical reality; occurring within history, conversion was against history as well, and the temporal story of the self was interrupted by its manifestation. "[A]s to the circumstances: is this change to be gradual or instantaneous?" George Henry queried rhetorically; then answered, "It is both the one and the other."[7]

The discourse of conversion and the creation of the narrative self operated within this dynamic matrix of history and myth. By constituting the narrative act of conversion as that which takes place in the liminal space between myth and history, the evangelical was able to mediate between them, universalizing what he claimed as personal experience and personalizing what he understood to be the meaningful order of the universe. A key element of concern in the conversion narratives was thus the sanctification of profane, historical time by reference to sacred, mythic time. It was a transformation that had to be done, necessarily, through language and metaphor; through the power of the discourse to constitute what it also described.

For many evangelical autobiographers, this discursive transformation was indicated by their inability to gauge the temporal process of their conversions. "How long I thus wrestled with the Lord," wrote John B. Hudson, "I know not"; and Ray Potter remarked that during his conversion experience he felt he was being transported into "eternity." Echoing Colton's description of the compressed temporality of the new birth, Ariel Kendrick commented, "In these few moments more knowledge of God, His law, the evil nature of sin, and the extreme enmity of my heart; was communicated to me, than ever before in my whole life." In a similar fashion, Elias Smith remarked in describing his conversion, "Though all these things were wrought in my mind at once, yet I could not distinguish them as afterwards." Smith's temporal confusion was compounded by a spatial one as well. "It is not possible for me to tell how long I remained in that situation," Smith wrote, "as everything earthly was gone from me for some time. . . . Looking around me, every object was changed."[8]

Even if conversion somehow took place apart from historical existence, only historical time gave coherence to the autobiographical construction of self; and many, if not most, evangelical autobiographers could be very specific in temporally locating their conversions, citing precise dates and even the exact time. For Peter Howell, his experience took place on "5th of September, 1824," and for Joshua Comstock, conversion occurred "on the 4th of August . . . about noon." Similarly, John B. Hudson noted that the "ever to be gratefully remembered event took place on the 20th of November, 1798, just before I had reached my 27th year," and Joseph Thomas recalled that his conversion occurred "[o]n the 7th of May, 1807, early in the morning."[9] Others used more equivocal language but clearly intended to express a similar certainty. "It was an hour never to be forgotten," observed Abner Chase. "May my sun of life set as cloudless and gently, as to me the material sun sunk away on that memorable evening." Freeborn Garrettson noted that his state of conviction continued until June 1775, on which date occurred, in his words, "The blessed morning I shall never forget! . . . I knew the very instant, when I submitted to the Lord, and was willing that Christ should reign over me." The Congregationalist pastor Elam Potter admitted his inability to be so temporally precise, but left no doubt as to the historical affirmation of his experience: "O blessed be the Lord for that memorable month (to me) of July, in the year 1764. That was the glorious year, that was the blessed month (though I cannot fix upon the day) in which I humbly hope salvation was brought to my soul."[10]

In spite of their conviction that conversion could be located within a specific and identifiable moment of time, the evangelicals shared with their Puritan predecessors a fear that the historical progression of time was also fatally damaging to the prospect of conversion. The danger of historical existence, even for Calvinists such as the Puritans, was made clear when it was juxtaposed with a mythic eternity. "Satan told me it was too late to pray," related one prospective member of Michael Wigglesworth's congregation. "My time was past[.] God had left me a long time [ago] and therefore there was little hopes [*sic*] he would return to me again." Historical time was irrecoverable, and this posed a fatal danger to the process of conversion—to reject the historical moment was to reject God. "I thought the time was past," remarked one of Thomas Shepard's parishioners; while another was thankful that God had helped him "part with sin and to redeem that time that I had formerly misspent."[11] Conversion could at least partially redeem for the loss of the past.

In a similar vein, evangelicals struggled to express their frustrations with historical time. "This view which I had of the solemn realities of the eternal world," wrote Ray Potter, "produced corresponding views of the shortness of time, and perishable nature of everything around me."[12] History was not redemptive, and the relentless progress and irrecoverable nature of historical time posed a dangerous threat to the possibility of conversion. "I found that holy time had always been a burden to me," wrote Elam Potter. But, "for near four weeks, it seemed I must make or break for eternity soon. I was ready to fear this was the last time that ever God would call." After his conversion, Potter wrote that he discouraged fellow students (and by extension his readers) from hesitating in this matter, ominously warning, "If this [conversion] is not done speedily, the time may soon be too late." Ann Judson recorded her fears about failing to "redeem the time" when she noted, "I often used to weep, when hearing the minister and others, press the importance of improving the present favorable season, to obtain an interest in Christ, lest we should have to say, *The harvest is past, the summer is ended, and we are not saved.*" For Harriet Livermore, not even her experience of conversion could remove her guilt at having squandered time: "I usually set up till past the midnight hour, and rose very early in the morning. I felt a very great anxiety to redeem the time, knowing I had lost the first score of years [prior to her conversion] allotted me by a merciful and kind Preserver." Freeborn Garrettson even recounted his conversion as a struggle against both God and time: "[A]t length [I] addressed my Maker thus: Lord, spare me one year more, and by that time I can put my worldly affairs in such a train, that I can serve thee . . . [but] the answer was, 'Now is the accepted time.' I then plead for six months, but was denied—one month, no—I then asked for one week, the answer was, 'This is the time.'"[13]

Few evangelical autobiographers, including those who presented themselves as otherwise orthodox Calvinists, seemed aware of the theological tension created between a redemptive process that took place outside of time and its manifestation within time. Missed opportunities for conversion assumed eternal consequence, even among those who continued to profess the doctrine of predestination. Solomon Mack, the maternal grandfather of the Mormon prophet Joseph Smith, warned his readers that delay was fraught with danger: "How often we hear, but do not obey him . . . , because we will say there is time enough yet, and I have something more to attend to of my worldly business. . . . I invite you to hearken to the calls that often presses into your minds, and put it not away for another day." Hosea Smith cautioned his readers "not to do as I have done—to strive against the holy spirit and to put those things off to a more convenient season, for the best time is the Lord's time." Although she ultimately obtained conversion, Jarena Lee related one instance in which an inopportune interruption almost cost her a chance at salvation and for which she offered a traditionally orthodox interpretation.

> During this state of mind [i.e., her conviction], while sitting near the fire one evening
> . . . a view of my distressed condition so affected my heart, that I could not refrain
> from weeping and crying aloud. . . . I arose from where I was sitting, being in an
> agony, and weeping convulsively, requested [another woman in the room] to pray
> for me; but at the very moment when she would have done so, some person rapped
> heavily at the door for admittance; . . . this occurrence was sufficient to interrupt us
> in our intentions; and I believe to this day, I should then have found salvation to
> my soul. This interruption was, doubtless, the work of Satan.[14]

The consequences of such delay, of course, were enormous. "I believe that many persons here," wrote Stephen H. Bradley, "in this christian land, have often had the Holy Spirit striving with them when they were young, and they have stifled their convictions, and perhaps they will continue to do so, until God may say that his spirit shall strive with them no longer, and if this should be done, they will be given over to hardness of heart and blindness of mind, and then they may expect to go to hell."[15]

While the danger of hell was no doubt understood quite literally by evangelical autobiographers, it was also a way of giving expression to the fall into the meaninglessness of purely historical existence. The only meaningful time of redemption was transcendent and transhistorical. Historical time—and by extension the historical narrative self—was without ultimate meaning but was, paradoxically, the sole modality through which the eternal redemptive activity of God could be realized. In their conversion narratives, evangelicals attempted to resolve this dilemma, and the language of conversion allowed them to mediate between these dialectical temporal demands. "I now felt the necessity of attending to the all-important concerns of eternity," wrote Asa Wild of his preconversion convictions. "I saw that life was but for a moment; that time was a vapour; that I was fast hastening to the tomb, and already stood on the borders of eternity."[16]

If time existed in a double mode within the narratives, so did space; and as the earlier quotations from Nancy Towle and Ray Potter illustrate, there is a specific "geography of conversion" to be found in evangelical autobiography. Conversion presented not just a temporal concern but also a spatial one that often involved some sort of narrative removal of the author from one place to another. Such narrative wandering became a metaphor used by many autobiographers to further underscore their personal agency in choosing conversion. Physical movement was an important theme in the narratives of Solomon Mack, Levi Hathaway, and Joshua Comstock. For Peter Howell, conversion was compared to a journey of walking along a creek "upon slippery and dangerous rocks," and Elam Potter struck a more conventional note when he proposed "to set out and take my journey towards the heavenly Zion."[17] Like their Puritan forebears who sought the temporal assurance of salvation by physical moment across the English countryside or even to America, evangelical spiritual autobiographers traversed the landscapes of two intersecting geographic realms that correlated to the division of the narrative self. The first of these might be termed the "historical landscape," wherein the landmarks of the natural and human world traced the author's actual physical movement through space. The other, and more important, geographic concern of the accounts was the "mythic landscape," which transformed the historical geography into a metaphor for the author's spiritual pilgrimage. "I had travelled East, West, North, and South, to find happiness in this world, but had not found it," Levi Hathaway lamented, recounting his journeys from New England to western Pennsylvania and back again. "My desire now is to find a path that leads to heaven and happiness."[18]

If movement was a metaphor for seeking conversion, then "rest" was its opposite. Peter Howell, for example, compared his preconversion journeys with the state of his soul, which even "in retired moments . . . was sometimes like the troubled ocean, that cannot rest." Ray Potter wrote, "I was overwhelmed with horror—I knew not where to flee—I could see nothing permanent or substantial on which I could rest." Billy Hibbard reported hearing the voice of Christ say to him, "Be faithful unto death and this shall be thy place of rest."[19] Others were less direct in their description of conversion as rest, but their more consciously metaphorical references could be strikingly powerful and evocative. Elam Potter noted his conversion occurred only after he came to the resolution "[t]hat I would venture all upon the seas for Christ; though my bark was slender, and the seas rough with storms and rocks, yet I was constrained to push off, and venture all, one time, to go to Christ." His subsequent conversion and experience of the "glory" of God induced him to "lay down" because he "could hold no more." For J. W. Holman, water was a placid rather than chaotic metaphor, though equally dynamic: "the ocean of God's love, rolled over my soul, and my load of iniquity sunk in a moment in the bottomless sea! Wave after wave, in sweet succession crossed my heart, and filled my soul with serenity and peace."[20] The account of Solomon Mack was particularly impressive in this regard. Describing his entire preconversion life as a series of failed and ultimately futile activities as a soldier, merchant, farmer, and speculator, Mack described his final journey toward conversion as occurring only when rheumatism confined him to his bed at the age of seventy-eight. There, he recalled, "the 11th Chapter of Matthew, and 28th to the 30th verses came to my mind. . . .[:] come unto me all ye that labor and are he[a]vy laden, and I will give you rest; take my yoke upon you, and learn of me, for I am meek and lowly in heart, and ye shall find rest unto your souls, for my yoke is easy and my burthen is light."[21] Mack immediately followed this scriptural allusion with a discussion of his own desecration of the Sabbath, which, as a symbol of sacred rest, stood in stark contrast to his own preconversion life of activity and ignorance of conversion. "I was in great distress," he recounted, "I could not sleep and took to reading; I was distressed to think how I had abused the Sabbath." Finally, after many sleepless nights, Mack prayed for relief from the physical pain he was experiencing, and was granted his first night of "rest" in his experience of conversion.[22]

The geography of conversion was thus conceived in both literal and metaphorical terms in the evangelical narratives, often occurring as the procurement of "rest" at the end of a "physical" movement through the historical landscape. This movement of the self through the narrative generated the dramatic structure of conversion and paralleled very clearly the evolution of conversion within the developing tradition of revivalism. Rooted in the Puritan practice of offering regular public expressions of "owning" or "renewing" the covenant bonds of the community and Scottish sacramental festivals,[23] revivalism began to take definitive shape in the 1740s under the leadership of Jonathan Edwards, George Whitefield, and the Tennent family in New Jersey, among others. The transatlantic "Great Awakening" of the mid-eighteenth century marked the maturation of revivalism as a mass ritual expression of Anglo-Protestant pietism that was "focused upon conversion and characterized by a highly charged emotional and physical, supposedly spontaneous, response."[24] Although revivalism remained a fluid and usually localized movement throughout the latter part of the eighteenth century, by the early nineteenth century it was rapidly becoming established as the most significant feature of evangelical ritual activity.

The great frontier revivals that occurred at the turn of the century, epitomized by Barton Stone's gathering at Cane Ridge, originated what would soon become a standard component of the revivalist's arsenal. With the development of the "altar area" or the "mourner's bench," the ritual structures of revivalism began to incorporate actual physical movement into the conversion process. As a specially designated area directly in front of the pulpit, the altar was "separated from the congregation and the pulpit, where sinners under conviction were brought to experience conversion."[25] According to the contemporary observer Calvin Colton, an "altar call" took place "ordinarily towards the close of the meeting," at which time "a challenge is formally made on all those, who are willing publicly to signify their anxiety to secure an interest in the great salvation—to separate themselves, that public prayer may be offered in their behalf. . . . And the effect of this step on those who thus present themselves, ordinarily is a speedy conversion."[26] Methodist and Baptist historians alike claimed credit for this successful innovation, but its place within the revivalist tradition was assured only after the Presbyterian evangelist Charles G. Finney incorporated it into his "new measures" during his famous Rochester revival of 1830. "A few days after the conversion of Mrs. M———," Finney wrote, "I made a call, I think for the first time, upon all that class of persons whose convictions were so ripe that they were willing to renounce their sins and give themselves to God, to come forward to certain seats which I requested to be vacated, and offer themselves up to God, while we made them subjects of prayer."[27]

By physically and publicly separating themselves from the congregation (where, in some contexts, the seating order often reflected the racial and sexual segregation of the larger society) potential converts who entered the altar area entered a ritual space where the transformation of conversion could properly be effected before they returned to their seats and, symbolically, to their stations in life. With the adoption of this movement through space, evangelical conversionism had come to typify a rite of passage, characterized by the separation, transformation, and reaggregation of the convert away from and back into the society.[28]

While such ritual separation, transformation, and social reaggregation could be physically enacted in the setting of a revival or camp meeting, it posed a discursive problem for evangelical autobiographers who needed to incorporate such significant movement within their presentations of conversion. That is to say, the author, as a character, had to ritually "move" through the narrative in a way that paralleled the ritual movement of conversion. The narratives had to reflect not only the temporal process of conversion, but also engage the author within a proper geography of conversion.

The obvious solution to this problem was simply to place one's conversion within the context of a revival, but few evangelical autobiographers chose this option. Both Peter Howell and Peter Cartwright admitted that their conversions took place during a camp meeting, and the Baptist elder John Peak placed his conversion in a room with a few friends immediately following a religious service, but most autobiographers located their conversions apart from even such incidentally communal contexts.[29] Many vehemently denied acquaintance with revivalist techniques or even knowledge of revival activity. Harriet Livermore insisted, "I never witnessed a revival of religion till after I was converted"; Ray Potter claimed that he also "never knew anything about a revival of religion" prior to his conversion; and according to David Marks, "No revival marked the period of my conversion and public profession of the same."[30] Such denials of the message and forms of evangelical religion may be read as simply conforming to the pattern demanded for the author's preconversion life—such as Solomon Mack's allegation that the master to whom he was apprenticed kept him "totally ignorant of Divine Revelation; or any thing appertaining to the christian religion" during his youth—but the often adamant obstinacy of evangelical autobiographers to acknowledge a revivalist or other formalized worship setting for their conversions forced them to construct other expressions for the ritual movement of the narrative self.[31]

"Almost as long ago as I can remember," recalled James Hooper, "I used to go alone and pray"; and similar acts of intentional seclusion and segregation are echoed in the vast majority of evangelical narratives.[32] So pervasive is this element that its presence must be attributed to discursive necessity rather than "factual" accuracy. "I well remember the place where I prayed," recounted the Methodist minister Elbert Osborn. "It was in a retired spot, in the open air; and it was on a cloudy sabbath morning when I trust that I was first enabled to rejoice through Christ Jesus in the light of God's reconciled countenance." Freeborn Garrettson explained that prior to his experience, "I lived a retired life, I frequently read, prayed, and wept till after midnight: and often withdrew to the woods, and other private places for prayer." Sounding again the theme of activity and rest, John B. Hudson recorded: "I repaired to the field but could not work[; thus,] . . . I withdrew to a more secluded spot, and cast myself prostrate on the ground."[33]

The theme of solitude was a symbol for sacrality, and the movement of the narrative self from ordinary or profane existence was balanced by his or her entry into a sacred space of potential encounter with God. The solitary locale became for the author a rhetorical setting for the revelation of the divine, and in the narratives such physical space could be discursively transformed into sacred space. Elam Potter noted that he often retired to a "solitary field" to pray and meditate alone, and Joshua Comstock expressed his desire "to be secluded from all society." Even John Peak's conversion while surrounded by his friends only culminates a lengthy period of seclusion and withdrawal. Peak notes that during conviction he had received religious impressions when alone in a field, in a room by himself, and while reading the Bible by himself on a Sabbath morning.[34] In the narrative absence of a revival structure with its clearly defined altar area, the woods, a lonely road, or even the more ambiguous "remote places" became liminal locations of transition and inversion.

Evangelical autobiographers no doubt intended such locales to represent the actual landscapes in which their conversions occurred, but they clearly recognized the metaphorical significance of such places as well. There were, of course, literary and biblical parallels to such a metaphoric reading of the landscape. James Champlin looked to *Pilgrim's Progress* and commented that under conviction, "in order to give vent to my feelings, I sought the solitary wood, or the secret closet, to pour out my soul before the Lord. . . . I now, like the pilgrim spoken of by Bunyan, knew not where to fly." For Charles Giles, his process of separation, which began during his family's move away from his childhood home, was nothing short of a biblical exile. "The thought that I must leave the place where I had spent my days of childhood, filled my mind with gloom and anxiety," he wrote. "That rural spot was my Eden—the peaceful centre of the world to me."[35] The disruption and separation from his childhood home led him eventually to conversion. Such overt biblical references were surprisingly rare in the evangelical autobiographies, although the concept of the "wilderness" as a place of separation and transformation—which may itself be regarded as a biblical theme—was common. In placing his preconversion conviction subsequent to his family's move to the Vermont countryside, Abner Jones wrote that "to return to the situation of my mind . . . I know not a better similitude than the wilderness in which I then dwelt, uncultivated, and inhabited by the wild beasts of prey; dreary and melancholy." Preconversion conviction and desire for conversion was described by Abner Chase in similar spatial imagery: "I therefore longed for this, as one panting for cooling waters, in a parched and thirsty land." Henry Holcombe commented concerning his period of conviction, "I pressed for the lonely desert, and without moving my tongue, or raising my eyes, abandoned myself to black despair, and the unrelenting severity of my guilty conscience. . . . I again broke the silence of the solitary place in which I was [by crying out]."[36] Others avoided such explicit identification of the geography of their conviction/conversion with wilderness or desert, but nevertheless described the natural surrounding as a place of special dread and fear. "It seemed as if all nature was dying around me. . . . I could see no beauty in anything around me, for the world had lost its charms, all creation seemed dying," wrote Ray Potter. For David Marks, "Nature itself wore a solemn gloom, and even the trees seemed to mourn, and the heavens to frown."[37]

While male autobiographers such as Potter and Marks usually recounted a movement "outward" into a solitary and despoiled natural setting such as "the solitary wood" or even "the lonely road," female autobiographers usually moved into more "interior" or domestic settings. Ann Judson recounted, "I shut myself up in my chamber, denied myself every innocent gratification; such as eating fruit and other things, not absolutely necessary to support life, and spent my days in reading and crying for mercy" for some two to three weeks prior to conversion. In similar fashion, Harriet Livermore was converted alone in her chamber, in a corner, behind a locked door. The African American autobiographer Zilpha Elaw was working as a domestic servant at the time of her conversion, which she placed in the isolated setting of a barn. "[A]t the time when this occurrence [conversion] took place," she wrote, "I was milking in the cow stall; and the manifestation of his [Christ's] presence was so clearly apparent, that even the beast of the stall turned her head and bowed herself upon the ground. Oh, never, never, shall I forget the scene."[38] Only a few male autobiographers placed their conversion within such a domestic setting. Richard Lee was converted in a biblically allusive "upper chamber" at home. James Hooper noted his being "a room by myself" when his conversion occurred; significantly he had just left his father behind mowing in a field.[39]

Whether depicted as natural or manufactured, the narrative setting was always permeated with a sense of sacrality that was disclosed during the author's description of conversion. Although conversion was itself ineffable, the narrative transformation of the physical locale clearly provided them with an expressive metaphor. While this expression often included descriptions of special auditory or visual phenomenon, evangelical autobiographers usually warned that such experiences were not to be taken literally, but rather were symbolic of the sacrality of the locale. For David Marks, the gloominess of nature was suddenly transformed, "though the darkness of night veiled the earth, yet nature assumed a new aspect." J. W. Holman wrote that "nature seemed dressed in her beautiful robes." Similarly, for Billy Hibbard, who had described the natural world as "more dismal than a mourning shroud" prior to his conversion, he afterward commented, "I thought now I shall see no more trouble for ever, for the Lord has made the world over anew."[40] Others described the locale of their conversions as an *axis mundi,* or threshold through which the mythical three-tiered universe could be glimpsed and traversed. The solitary place became a limen that joined the profane and sacred worlds, allowing the autobiographer—and the reader—to perceive a larger reality than could be contained in the mere physical setting. "I was instantly surrounded with a divine power," wrote Freeborn Garrettson. "[H]eaven and hell were disclosed to view, and life and death were set before me." Echoing Garrettson, Ray Potter commented that "heaven and hell were alike to me," and Nathan Noyes asserted that "[h]eaven and hell appeared in my view." For James Champlin, conversion not only changed him, but also transfigured the landscape: "the transports of joy with which my thoughts were filled gave everything around me the appearance of a paradise," he recounted.[41] In their descriptions of this state of liminality, autobiographers were able to rhetorically remove themselves from profane existence and place themselves, as characters, into a sacred and unearthly locale.

As Barton Stone had commented about the conversion accounts he heard in his adolescence in the Virginia backcountry, converts often reported their conversions were influenced by visions, dreams, and other visual or auditory phenomena. "I prayed for an evidence," wrote Baptist autobiographer Hosea Smith. "I lay and looked out of the window—I thought I never saw it look so pleasant in all my life before. I thought I heard the most beautiful singing that I ever heard in my life." Similarly, Nathan Noyes reported a biblically inspired vision of the twenty-four elders audibly praising God around the heavenly throne. "This I thought was too much for a mere mortal to see, and hear," he wrote. "[T]herefore, I began to conclude it was not real, it was only my imagination. I was told to listen, and if it was not real, there would be many jars, and much discord; but if it was real, all this music would be in harmony. To my great surprise, when I had listened a while, all those notes, or sounds, which were made by those heavenly beings, appeared to be a perfect concord. This convinced me it was real, and no phantom or delusion." Zilpha Elaw offered a lengthy description of her vision of Christ as "a tall figure" with "long hair, which parted in the front and came down on his shoulders," wearing "a long white robe down to the feet." "I might have tried to imagine, or persuade myself, perhaps, that it had been a vision presented merely to the eye of my mind," she explained, "but, the beast of the stall gave forth her evidence to the reality of the heavenly appearance; for she turned her head and looked round as I did; and when she saw, she bowed her knees and cowered upon the ground."[42]

Despite Noyes's and Elaw's professed verification of their experiences, most autobiographers were careful to circumscribe such visual and auditory experiences as being real only in a personal sense. "I thought I saw the Saviour, by faith, in human shape, for about one second in the room, with arms extended, appearing to say to me, come," Stephen H. Bradley reported; and Ray Potter imagined himself "standing before the awful throne of God" and further qualified his report by adding that "in fact, my *mind* was there." The Methodist autobiographer William Keith was even more careful to offer a more theological explication for his vision. "On a sudden, as if by divine impulse," he wrote, "I was filled with such a sense of the presence of God, that I as firmly believed that he was all around me as if I could have seen him visibly before me. I then for the first time understood that God, though a spirit invisible to us, fills immensity of space."[43] Billy Hibbard's account of "seeing" both God and Christ during his conversion was especially ambiguous:

> I saw Jesus Christ at the right hand of God looking down upon me, and God the Father looking upon him. The look of Jesus on me removed the burden of my sins, while he spoke these words, "Be faithful unto death and this shall be thy place of rest." I never had seen Jesus Christ before, nor heard his voice, nor ever had a sense of his intercession at the right hand of God for me till now. . . . Beholding the glory of God by faith, was a rapturous sight; but soon it was suggested that I must open my eyes on creation. . . . I opened my eyes therefore, while still on my knees: and behold all nature was praising God. The sun and firmament, the trees, birds, and beasts, all appeared stamped with the glory of God. . . . If I had kept my eyes open, I should not have seen God in glory, and Jesus Christ, which was the best of all.[44]

Hibbard's careful wording here and the fact that these things were "seen" only while his eyes were closed suggests that the description of his conversion was to be understood as evocative, not literal. In fact, despite some exceptions, most evangelical autobiographers emphasized that such descriptions were to be read as rhetorical devices, not as factual verities. While their function in the text was to indicate the significance of conversion, visions and other strange phenomenon were rarely offered as evidences of conversion, and many autobiographers suffered through additional periods of hesitation and doubt before they reported assurance of their conversions. As expressed by Charles Giles, his conversion was accompanied by a revelation of a straight road to heaven surrounded by a dark desert as well as words of comfort and reassurance spoken to him by an angel. "All this I believed was only a wakeful, ideal vision, which passed before the eye of my mind at the time," he wrote. While he was willing to grant that "it might have been the effect of some supernatural agency," he was careful to disassociate the assurance of his conversion from this imagined insight into the nature of things. "These views," wrote Giles, "did not constitute any part of the foundation of my Christian hope. Benevolent feelings, love to God and his cause, a concern for the souls of my fellow-mortals, together with the peace, assurance, and faith which I felt, at the time, formed the basis of my hope. These evidences, to my conscious mind, possessed the power and attributes of a reality."[45]

Giles's account of his conversion underscored the reluctance many autobiographers expressed in placing too much emphasis on such visionary elements for their evidence and assurance of salvation. Rather than depend upon such individual and subjective experiences, it was only in the final ritual movement back into society, into the discursive community, that the transformation of the author was complete. Giles's "benevolent feelings" and "concern for the souls of my fellow-mortals" were the touchstones of his experience and could only be activated in his return, as a convert, to human society.

From the progressively narrowing focus upon the separated self in the preconversion section of the narrative, which culminated in most narratives with total social isolation of the self at the moment of conversion, this final movement of ritual transformation redirected the convert back into society and endowed him or her with a special regard for others. Such an attitude of "communitas" was a marked feature of virtually every evangelical narrative and was directed toward the convert's full incorporation into the discursive community and reincorporation into the society at large.[46] Ann

Judson explicitly used this metaphor of movement and transformation in her account. "I now began to hope," she wrote of her conversion, "that I had passed from death unto life. When I examined myself, I was constrained to own, that I had feelings and dispositions, to which I was formerly an utter stranger. I had sweet communion with the blessed God, from day to day; my heart was drawn out in love to Christians of whatever denomination." Eleazer Sherman observed, "I never enjoyed such exquisite happiness in all my life: my love extended to the whole world, and I felt as though I had not an enemy on the earth," adding, "Christian people were as dear to me as my own relatives."[47] Stephen H. Bradley recounted his conversation with a deacon in the moments following his conversion: "I went to the fire-place, where one of the Deacons of the Church sat conversing, and told him with trembling, that I thought I loved christians, and he made this reply to me, 'We know that we have passed from death unto life, because we love the brethren.' . . . I had an ardent desire, that all mankind might feel as I did, I wanted to have them all love God supremely. Previous to this time, I was so very selfish and self-righteous, that I cared but little about the welfare of others; but now I desired the welfare of all mankind."[48]

Beyond society, even nature itself, which prior to conversion had been such a setting of gloom and despair, was narratively transfigured during conversion. "The world of nature now appeared all new. The wilderness and the solitary place now indeed displayed their gladness," wrote John B. Hudson. Abner Chase commented that "all nature seemed to smile with joy, which perfectly chimed in with the calm which had just come over my soul." Hosea Smith framed a similar observation within the Pauline metaphor of the new creation: "It seemed to me that everything was praising God—old things had passed away and all things had become new. I loved every body and thought that every body was my friend."[49]

Such sentiments might be easily dismissed as conventional and formulaic were it not for the tension that they engendered with the image of humility that conversion accounts were supposed to reflect. Not only did such expressions move the convert back into relationship with others, but they also made the "converted self" the fulcrum of these relationships. Rather than extinguish the self, conversion Christianized the self and made the autobiographer an exemplar of true faith. For Freeborn Garrettson, this took the form of a new dispensation of primitive Christianity, manifested

THE LANGUAGE OF THE SACRED · 83

corporately in the advent of Methodism but personally in Garrettson's own sanctity as an exemplar of Christian piety.[50] Theophilus Gates was even more transparent in his assumption of a Christlike identity, apparently unaware of how this contrasted with the evangelical ideal of humility and self-abnegation.

[I] had such a sight of the wisdom of God in the plan of salvation; and felt such a love in my heart towards him and all mankind, as can never be expressed by words, nor any one have any idea of, unless they have experienced it themselves. . . . I felt willing to die for the sake of Christ; yea, and to be everlastingly miserable myself to make every body else happy. I was as nothing in my own sight. . . . And such love did I feel for all mankind, and such compassion had I towards them from a sense of the bondage they were under to sin, and their unhappy situation, that I felt willing to die for a single fellow creature; yea, if consistent with the will of God, and it were possible, I wanted, from my heart, and could not but pray, that the afflictions and miseries of all mankind might be laid upon me, and I bear them myself to all eternity, for the sake of making them all completely and for ever happy. . . . I had such a love to others that I cared not what became of myself if they all could be happy; and I felt such displeasure, yea, hatred against myself, for my past ingratitude to God and the evil of my nature, that I delighted most in the greatest sufferings.[51]

In another place and time, such apotheosis might be read as blasphemous, but in the spiritual autobiographies it only defined the requisite end of the evangelical discourse of self. The self was transformed through the performative function of the text itself in a "conversion" that was completed only with the narrative movement of the self into the discursive community. Conversion was thus not merely a theological or ecclesiastical claim; it was a rhetorical activity that occurred within the context of the narrative that configured both self and community. Through their use of a canonical "language of the sacred," evangelical autobiographers constructed a world of meaning in which the autonomous self, as a literary subject, could be redeemed "literally" by its ritual movement through the text.

New ritual formulations develop when situations arise that threaten to disrupt the accepted encodations of meaning within a given society. Clearly, the revivalism of early evangelicalism provided one such means of ritual response to the tensions of early modern culture. As William G. McLoughlin argued, the "Great Awakenings" fostered by early American evangelicals, with their emphasis on revivalistic activity, provided a means of "cultural revitalization" intended "to overcome jarring disjunctions between norms and experience, old beliefs and new realities, dying patterns and emerging patterns of behavior."[52] As a discursive mechanism for deconstructing the old and thus allowing for the emergence of the new, spiritual autobiographies performed a similar sort of personal as well as cultural catharsis for American evangelicals. The same forms and structures of ritual movement found in the revivals were replicated in the autobiographies where evangelicals overcame the problems of the modern self by making themselves both the subjects and objects of conversion discourse.

CONCLUSION

In the previous chapters, I have attempted to read the spiritual autobiographies of early American evangelicals corporately rather than individually, in contradistinction to most studies of American autobiography. My intention, of course, was to examine the generic parameters of the evangelical discourse of conversion rather than to indicate the way in which specific autobiographers presented themselves as converts. The discursive elements that I have identified and discussed, however, were certainly not invariable, and each autobiographer adopted the various elements in diverse ways. As Peter Stromberg observed, the writing of a conversion narrative allowed the author to integrate "a shared religious language into the idiosyncratic details of their own life histories and situations";[1] and so to read the spiritual autobiographies and conversion narratives of early American evangelicalism as unimaginative attempts merely to replicate the morphologies of the theologians fails to recognize the necessary creativity by which their authors engaged in this integration of the demands of both modern autobiography and discourse. There is no "typical" evangelical spiritual autobiography in that "the idiosyncratic details" of the life of a single autobiographer were, like the self they presented, not easily conformed to ideal patterns. Through the examination of a specific text, however, we might glimpse some of the ways in which evangelical authors struggled to conform the unruly self of history into the larger motifs of discursive meaning.

As he lay dying in 1806, James Ireland dictated his spiritual autobiography to an unnamed scribe who published the volume some thirteen years later. Although Ireland worried that "[t]his circumstance [of dictation] will ... render the relation more incorrect, and the chain of events less connected than they otherwise might have been," he hoped nonetheless that the work would fulfill his desire "to give a just relation of the wonderful dealings of a gracious God to me a sinner."[2] But if providing a proper paradigm for conversion was his only professed goal, it was not the only effect of the autobiography. In adopting the language of evangelical conversion, Ireland found a way to speak about himself that gained not only the endorsement but also the approval of the evangelical community. The completed work placed Ireland's conversion at its very center; a fitting symbol of the centrality of conversion in the life of the evangelical. From this vantage point, Ireland, as author and character, could view, organize, and interpret his experiences. The linguistic structure that he employed did much more than replicate the pietistic formula of despair, conviction, and conversion—it enabled Ireland to speak of himself, and indeed to create a meaningful and coherent self through the agency of conversion discourse.

Like all evangelical autobiographers of the early modern age, Ireland struggled with the demands of pietistic orthodoxy and the exigencies of history. Accounts of his birth and childhood, "customary," in his words, "when the history of a person's life is published" (7), were necessary evils to fulfill his task. But try as he might to follow the pietistic prescription that speaks of self-annihilation, Ireland could not help but proclaim himself all the more as an autonomous being whose life could not be confined to the mythic ideal of conversion. In writing about his attempts to realize conversion, Ireland commented that "herein lay my error; I was engaged to produce and perform that act myself" (104). Yet there was no other way.

Ireland was born in 1748 in Scotland and was old enough to remember the visit of George Whitefield to his native city of Edinburgh. Although his father experienced conversion as a result of Whitefield's preaching, Ireland refused to linger over it in his narrative, explaining to his readers, "I am not writing the history of his life, but that of my own, [and] I shall add no more on the subject" (14). Although he claimed that his own encounter with Whitefield had little impact on his life, by his own account his was a rather conservative Scottish Presbyterian childhood. His parents, at least after his father's conversion, seem to have been active Christians, and Ireland noted the "approbation" he received from family and friends for his skills in learning his catechism. Even such a conventionally religious and moral life, however, was cause for censure: "I can now reflect back and see that, from this source," he wrote, "I imbibed a tolerable degree of pharisaical pride" (10). Pride, indeed, was a problem, but Ireland was trapped within a dialectic that enjoined him to profess humility while at the same time present his experience as a paradigm for emulation. While he warned his readers against mistaking morality for true piety, he nonetheless recounted, "From my parents instruction and encouragement, I imbibed a hatred against taking the name of God in vain," and reported on his distribution of food to beggars on the basis of his having heard the parable of the rich man and Lazarus (12–13). But conversion could not come through such pious acts of charity, and Ireland's narrative presents his preconversion life as a progressive pilgrimage into the isolation and solitude from which his conversion would eventually issue.

Against the wishes of his family, Ireland quit his education to seek his fortune at sea, but an unspecified "juvenile indiscretion" led finally to his emigration to America in order to escape legal penalty. Unlike the Puritans for whom immigration was such a crucial metaphor for conversion, Ireland generally resisted the metaphorical possibilities of this experience.[3] He did relate one experience of a hurricane encountered at sea, commenting, "It is not my design, to swell the relation of this narrative with every circumstance of danger that I have escaped . . . but I cannot help recording some imminent dangers through which I have been brought, in order to set forth the wonderful goodness of God" (32–33). For the most part, the account of his immigration was only one more marker in his growing separation from his former being.

Ireland's arrival in northern Virginia in the early 1760s coincided with an outbreak of a revivalistic fervor there led by the also recently arrived Separate Baptists. In spite of the fact that Ireland claims to have "entertained the most violent prejudices against" the Separates, making a vow at one point never to become a Baptist (71), it is clear that the presentation he makes of his irreligious lifestyle are exaggerated. "Although I had little of the fear of God before my eyes if any," he wrote of his arrival in Virginia, "yet from the benefit of an early education and parental instruction, together with the practice of those amongst whom I had lived, I felt some degree of reverence for the lords day." Influenced by a similar reverence exemplified by nearby Quakers, Ireland continued his ritual separation—"it disposed me to take my Bible and retire into the woods by myself" (44–45).

Ireland's proclaimed rejection of the Separates, however, soon proves to be rhetorical. Only after recounting the gradual and apparently independent growth of his convictions does he inform his readers that in fact he had been attending Separate religious services for over a year (70–71). From this point on, Ireland's progressive separation and eventual return to community (represented by the Separates) forms the predominant theme of his conversion account. In journeying to America, Ireland abandoned an at least nominally religious childhood for the profane life that America represented. His conversion returned him both theologically to God and discursively to the community he had abandoned.

Ireland's increasing conviction of sin led him to further withdrawal and separation. This was marked in part by the abandonment of his former associates in sin who grew alarmed at Ireland's behavior and employed, as Ireland expressed it, "every artifice . . . to get me back to my old courses; but it could not avail," adding, "I was then almost continually in solitude and retirement in the woods" (76–77). This period of preconversion despair drove Ireland away from former companions, and his sylvan retreats essentially dehumanized him. "So vile I felt in my own sight that had strangers to religion accidentally come upon me at such times, when in the woods, and beheld me dropping to my knees, wringing my hands, . . . had they heard me mourning like a dove, and chattering like a swallow, they would have conceived me to be a person bereaved of his senses" (89).

"I felt myself at a loss in a measure to find language to convey a regular series of ideas of that complicated confusion and distress that I felt for two or three days" (72). Yet Ireland's language was the only means by which he was able eventually to order and interpret himself to himself. His conviction actually begins when a friend requests of him a poem on "the natural man's dependence on heaven" (59) and is deepened when he composes additional poems. This exercise, he observed, "was productive of a little contrition, and gave me a distant but feint hope, that God might at last be propitious to *me*" (75). Despite the conventional nature of the language employed, Ireland was able to use it to speak meaningfully of himself within a discursive context that allowed for such expression. "[W]hat I write now, is only my own experience," (93) he commented as began the description of his conversion experience.

At length, Ireland prepared himself for conversion and the denouement of his narrative. Although Ireland conceived conversion as coming "by grace through faith, and not of myself, for it was the gift of God," his account demonstrates the problematic issue of autonomy that evangelicals confronted but could not eliminate. "Under the influence of the ... scriptures," Ireland recalled, "I arose up out of bed, put on my clothes, went out into the woods a considerable distance, with a full resolution not to return back, until I had believed in Jesus Christ" (103). He spent this entire night alone, first in the woods then at a schoolhouse where he taught. The following morning, auspiciously the "Lord's day," Ireland concluded to go to hear a certain minister speak nearby and began his journey toward that destination (104).

Ireland does not mention whether or not the minister he went to hear was a Separate, but his earlier rejection of the Separates now becomes crucial in constructing his own conversion. Like the biblical Paul, who had originally persecuted Christians before his "conversion," Ireland has been presented (somewhat disingenuously) as a persecutor. Now his conversion, like that of his biblical counterpart, occurs while he is on the road.

> As I was walking down the main country road by myself, being pretty early, my present sensations according to the best of my recollections were as follows— I viewed and felt myself the most odious and poluted [*sic*] being existing. . . . I viewed God as an unreconciled God to me. . . . In this situation I descended a short declivity in the road, and when I arrived at the bottom, in a moment of time, there seemed like a voice from heaven, that echoed into my soul these words—"O love! O light! O glory!" I lost all remembrance of being upon earth, and something appeared to me, although not in a distinct manner, as if I was present with the happy spirits above. . . . I rose upon my feet [and] . . . all that pressure of sin and guilt that burdened my soul appeared to be removed and gone. (105)

The description is classic, and the setting, of course, was ideal. Ireland was alone and at his lowest point both literally and metaphorically. Upon conversion, the setting was transfigured and Ireland felt himself removed from his mundane existence—"so great was the peace and calm diffuse through my soul, that the transition almost seemed to great for nature to bear" (105–6). And although expressive of the significance of his conversion, Ireland was careful to describe it as emblematic and not "factual." The "voice" that he "heard" was symbolic of the presence of the sacred: "As I moved along, I viewed further, that the words that came to me, viz. love, light and glory, were expressive of the very being, essence and attributes of God" (106).

Regardless of the dramatic intensity of the account of his conversion, the process remained incomplete at this point in the narrative. Having ritually separated himself from human society, Ireland now needed to verify his experience through the agency of the discursive community. Although he did not abjure his experience on the road, it was followed by further despair until—continuing his metaphorical journey—he arrived at the home of a friend on "Massinottin mountain." There, in the growing presence of other friends that symbolized his entry back into society, Ireland was able to gain the proper perspective from which to view his experience. While praying with his friends, he recounted, "I was enabled then to take a retrospect back to that happy time (I have given a relation of) on the great road, and saw that *that* was the time when God *converted* my soul" (122). His full reintegration into society came with his acceptance of "believer's baptism by immersion" and his joining with the Separate Baptists, where he sought ordination as a minister. The remainder of his autobiography details his activities as a circuit-riding evangelist in Virginia's Shenandoah Valley and his service as the pastor of three small Baptist churches in the Ketocton Baptist Association.[4]

In his postconversion retrospection on his life, Ireland gave coherence and meaning to his experience and gained a voice through which he was able to present himself to the world. The literary structure he employed, however, was more than a rote formula of despair, conviction, and conversion. By admitting the autonomous self into the American consciousness, the discourse of evangelical conversion created an enduring paradigm of American literature, not by contributing a linguistic formula that would later be "secularized," but rather by creating a modernist discourse where the ambivalence and tensions of modern selfhood could be confronted.

Intentional or not, the primary achievement of the antebellum spiritual autobiographers was not to demonstrate the degree of correspondence between their experiences and a preordained morphology of conversion, but to locate themselves within a complex matrix of narrative space and time wherein they tried to resolve the dialectical tensions—between myth and history, self and community—by generating a new discourse of conversion.

NOTES

Chapter 1. The Discourse of Evangelical Conversion

1. William G. McLoughlin, *The American Evangelicals, 1800–1900: An Anthology* (Gloucester, Mass.: Peter Smith, 1976), 1.

2. Robert Baird, *Religion in America* (New York, 1844), 184; George M. Marsden, *Understanding Fundamentalism and Evangelicalism* (Grand Rapids: William B. Eerdmans, 1991), 1–2; Timothy P. Weber, "Premillennialism and the Branches of Evangelicalism," in *The Variety of American Evangelicalism,* ed. Donald W. Dayton and Robert K. Johnson (Knoxville: Univ. of Tennessee Press, 1991), 13–14; James Davison Hunter, *American Evangelicalism: Conservative Religion and the Quandary of Modernity* (New Brunswick, N.J.: Rutgers Univ. Press, 1983), 7.

3. Barton Warren Stone, *The Biography of Eld. Barton Warren Stone, Written by Himself: With Additions and Reflections by Elder John Rogers* (Cincinnati, 1847), 37–38.

4. F. Ernest Stoeffler, *Rise of Evangelical Pietism* (Leiden: E. J. Brill, 1965), 17. On the relation of evangelicalism to the affective pietism of the seventeenth and eighteenth centuries, see Ted A. Campbell, *The Religion of the Heart: A Study of European Religious Life in the Seventeenth and Eighteenth Centuries* (Columbia: Univ. of South Carolina Press, 1991); and Randall Balmer, "Eschewing the 'Routine of Religion': Eighteenth-Century Pietism and the Revival Tradition in America," in *Modern Christian Revivals,* ed. Edith L. Blumhofer and Randall Balmer (Urbana and Chicago: Univ. of Illinois Press, 1993), 1–16.

5. Jonathan Edwards, *Religious Affections,* ed. John E. Smith, vol. 2 of *The Works of Jonathan Edwards* (New Haven: Yale Univ. Press, 1959), 340–41, 391. Hereafter all references to the Yale edition of Edwards's writings will be cited as Edwards, *Works,* followed by volume and page numbers after each volume's initial citation.

6. Jonathan Edwards, "Miscellaneous Observations," in *The Works of President Edwards,* 10 vols. (New York, 1830), vol. 7:473. Hereafter, all references to the New York edition of Edwards's writings will be cited as Edwards, *Works of President Edwards,* followed by volume and page numbers after each volume's initial citation.

7. William James, *The Varieties of Religious Experience* (1902; rpt., New York: Penguin, 1982), chap. 9–10; Edwin Diller Starbuck, *The Psychology of Religion: An Empirical Study of the Growth of Religious Consciousness* (London, 1899; rpt., New York: Charles Scribner's Sons, 1908); Joseph F. Kett, "Growing Up in Rural New England, 1800–1840," in *Anonymous Americans: Explorations in Nineteenth-Century Social History,* ed. Tamara K. Hareven (Englewood Cliffs, N.J.: Prentice-Hall, 1971), 11; Jerald C. Brauer, "Conversion: From Puritanism to Revivalism," *Journal of Religion* 58 (1978): 227–43; G. Van der Leeuw, *Religion in Essence and Manifestation,* 2 vols. (Gloucester, Mass.: Peter Smith, 1967), chap. 79; Lewis R. Rambo, *Understanding Religious Conversion* (New Haven: Yale Univ. Press, 1993).

8. Michel Foucault, *The Archaeology of Knowledge,* trans. A. M. Sheridan-Smith (New York: Pantheon, 1972), 107.

9. Ibid., 41–42. Foucault's famous examples of the way in which "madness" became a discursive object in the early modern period include *Madness and Civilization: A History of Insanity in the Age of Reason,* trans. Richard Howard (New York: Pantheon, 1965); and *The Birth of the Clinic: An Archaeology of Medical Perception,* trans. A. M. Sheridan-Smith (New York: Vintage, 1973).

10. Clifford Geertz, *The Interpretation of Cultures* (New York: Basic Books, 1973), 93.

11. Ibid., 108.

12. Sydney E. Ahlstrom, *A Religious History of the American People,* 2 vols. (New Haven: Yale Univ. Press, 1972), chap. 25; William Breitenbach, "The Consistent Calvinism of the New Divinity Movement," *William and Mary Quarterly,* 3d ser., 41 (1984): 241–64; Joseph Conforti, *Samuel Hopkins and the New Divinity Movement: Calvinism, the Congregational Ministry, and Reform in New England Between the Great Awakenings* (Grand Rapids: Christian Univ. Press, 1981); Sidney E. Mead, *Nathaniel William Taylor, 1786–1858: A Connecticut Liberal* (Chicago: Univ. of Chicago Press, 1942).

13. Stephen Greenblatt, *Renaissance Self-Fashioning: From More to Shakespeare* (Chicago: Univ. of Chicago Press, 1980); Joan Webber, *The Eloquent "I": Style and Self in Seventeenth-Century Prose* (Madison: Univ. of Wisconsin Press, 1968); John O. Lyons, *The Invention of the Self: The Hinge of Consciousness in the Eighteenth Century* (Carbondale: Southern Illinois Univ. Press, 1978).

14. Hayden White, *Tropics of Discourse: Essays in Cultural Criticism* (Baltimore and

NOTES TO PAGES 8-12 · 95

London: Johns Hopkins Univ. Press, 1978), 2; cf. Foucault, *Archaeology of Knowledge,* 48–49.

15. The English term *conversion* comes from the common biblical words for the action of "turning," which were often used metaphorically to describe the proper response of human beings to the divine call for repentance and faith. See William L. Holladay, *The Root Sûbh in the Old Testament* (Leiden: E. J. Brill, 1958); Paul Aubin, *Le problème de la "conversion": Étude sur un term commun a l'Hellénisme et au Christianisme des trois premiers siècles* (Paris: Beauchesne et ses Fils, 1963); and Beverly Roberts Gaventa, *From Darkness to Light: Aspects of Conversion in the New Testament* (Philadelphia: Fortress Press, 1986). On the concept of conversion in Christian history, see A. D. Nock, *Conversion: The Old and the New in Religion from Alexander the Great to Augustine of Hippo* (London: Oxford Univ. Press, 1961); Karl F. Morrison, *Understanding Conversion* (Charlottesville and London: Univ. Press of Virginia, 1992); and Marilyn J. Harran, *Luther on Conversion: The Early Years* (Ithaca: Cornell Univ. Press, 1983).

16. Zilpha Elaw, *Memoirs of the Life, Religious Experience, Ministerial Travels and Labours of Mrs. Zilpha Elaw* (London, 1846), 98; cf. Anne C. Loveland, *Southern Evangelicals and the Social Order, 1800–1860* (Baton Rouge: Louisiana State Univ. Press, 1980), 24.

17. Daniel B. Shea Jr., *Spiritual Autobiography in Early America* (Princeton: Princeton Univ. Press, 1968), vii; Virginia Lieson Brereton, *From Sin to Salvation: Stories of Women's Conversions, 1800 to the Present* (Bloomington: Indiana Univ. Press, 1991), 16.

18. Edmund S. Morgan, *Visible Saints: The History of a Puritan Idea* (Ithaca: Cornell Univ. Press, 1963), 66.

19. Brereton, *From Sin to Salvation,* 18; Shea, *Spiritual Autobiography in Early America,* xi.

20. Gary L. Ebersole, *Captured by Texts: Puritan to Postmodern Images of Indian Captivity* (Charlottesville and London: Univ. Press of Virginia, 1995), 10–12; quote from page 11.

21. White, *Tropics of Discourse,* 7–12; Foucault, *Archaeology of Knowledge,* 48–49.

22. Stanley Fish, *Is There a Text in This Class? The Authority of Interpretive Communities* (Cambridge: Harvard Univ. Press, 1980), 171.

23. On the influence of conversionism on other American literary forms, see Robert F. Sayre, "Religious Autobiography," in *Encyclopedia of the American Religious Experience: Studies of Traditions and Movements,* ed. Charles H. Lippy and Peter W. Williams (New York: Charles Scribner's Sons, 1988), vol. 2:1225–28; Daniel A. Cohen, *Pillars of Salt, Monuments of Grace: New England Crime Literature and the Origins of American Popular Culture, 1674–1860* (New York: Oxford Univ. Press, 1993), 13–14 and chap.

2–3; Alden T. Vaughan and Edward W. Clark, *Puritans Among the Indians: Accounts of Captivity and Redemption* (Cambridge: Belknap Press of the Harvard Univ. Press, 1981), 4; William L. Andrews, *To Tell a Free Story: The First Century of Afro-American Autobiography, 1760–1865* (Urbana and Chicago: Univ. of Illinois Press, 1986), 7; and Ebersole, *Captured by Texts,* 20. On the lack of generic models for conversion literature, see the comments of Peter G. Stromberg, *Language and Self-Transformation: A Study of the Christian Conversion Narrative* (Cambridge: Cambridge Univ. Press, 1993), 56; and Brereton, *From Sin to Salvation,* xi and 127, n.1.

Chapter 2. Evangelical Pietism and the Subjective Impulse

1. Foucault referred to this as the "author-function," which has less to do with the particularity of the individual writing than with the activity of the author as a unifying principle within the discourse. See Michel Foucault, "What Is an Author?" in *Textual Strategies: Perspectives in Post-Structuralist Criticism,* ed. Josué V. Harari (Ithaca: Cornell Univ. Press, 1979), 148–53, and "Discourse on Language," trans. Rupert Swyer, in Foucault, *Archaeology of Knowledge*, 221–22.
2. Cf. Foucault, "Discourse on Language," 216.
3. Foucault, *Archaeology of Knowledge,* 50–55.
4. Freeborn Garrettson, *The Experience and Travels of Mr. Freeborn Garrettson* (Philadelphia, 1791), iv–v.
5. Elias Smith, *The Life, Conversion, Preaching, Travels, and Sufferings of Elias Smith* 1 (Portsmouth, N.H., 1816), iii (no subsequent volumes were published).
6. Foucault, *Archaeology of Knowledge,* 51.
7. Jerome Hamilton Buckley, *The Turning Key: Autobiography and the Subjective Impulse since 1800* (Cambridge: Harvard Univ. Press, 1984), 19.
8. Wilhelm Dilthey, *Pattern and Meaning in History: Thoughts on History and Society,* ed. H. P. Rickman (New York: Harper, 1961), 85. Dilthey proposed to inaugurate a new system of "human studies" that would counter the excessive positivism of Auguste Comte by using the "lived experience" of individuals—best recorded in autobiographies—as its foundation.
9. Jean Starobinski, "The Style of Autobiography," in *Autobiography: Essays Theoretical and Critical,* ed. James Olney (Princeton: Princeton Univ. Press, 1980), 78.
10. On the rise of autobiography in the West, see James Olney, "Autobiography and the Cultural Moment: A Thematic, Historical, and Bibliographical Introduction," in Olney, *Autobiography,* 3–27.

11. Patricia Cox, *Biography in Late Antiquity: A Quest for the Holy Man* (Berkeley and Los Angeles: Univ. of California Press, 1983).

12. George Lyons, *Pauline Autobiography: Toward a New Understanding,* vol. 73 of Society of Biblical Literature Dissertation Series (Atlanta: Scholars Press, 1985), 36–53.

13. Edwin Goodenough, *The Theology of Justin Martyr: An Investigation into the Conceptions of Early Christian Literature and Its Hellenistic and Judaistic Influences* (Jena, 1923; rpt., Amsterdam: Philo Press, 1968), 63; Nock, *Conversion,* 107–10, 254–56.

14. Herbert Musurillo, *The Acts of the Christian Martyrs* (Oxford: Clarendon Press, 1972), l–lxii; Thomas J. Hefferman, *Sacred Biography: Saints and Their Biographers in the Middle Ages* (New York: Oxford, 1988); Morrison, *Understanding Conversion,* 41.

15. Buckley, *The Turning Key,* 20.

16. Paul Lehmann, "Autobiography in the Middle Ages," *Transactions of the Royal Historical Society,* 5th ser., 3 (1953): 42; Pierre Courcelle, *Les Confessions de saint Augustine dans le tradition littéraire: Antécédents et postérité* (Paris: Études Augustiniennes, 1963).

17. Too many studies of conversion have simply assumed that the experiences of Paul as recorded by the author of Acts, the *Confessions* of Augustine, and the conversion accounts of modern Protestant pietists are all describing the same type of experience for the same type of reasons (e.g., Peter A. Dorsey, *Sacred Estrangement: The Rhetoric of Conversion in Modern American Autobiography* [University Park: The Pennsylvania State Univ. Press, 1993], chap. 1). Despite the influence that the "conversion" of Paul may have had on the later evangelical mind, it was not, in the words of Krister Stendahl, "that inner experience of conversion which Western theology has taken for granted"; Krister Stendahl, *Paul Among Jews and Gentiles and Other Essays* (Philadelphia: Fortress Press, 1976), 12. Much the same argument can be made for *Confessions.*

18. Elizabeth W. Bruss, *Autobiographical Acts: The Changing Situation of a Literary Genre* (Baltimore: Johns Hopkins Univ. Press, 1976), 34.

19. William Haller, *The Rise of Puritanism* (New York: Columbia Univ. Press, 1938), 96.

20. J[ohn] B[eadle], *The Journal or Diary of a Thankful Christian, Presented in Some Meditations upon Numb. 33.2* (London, 1652), 48, 60, 102. I have modernized the spelling and punctuation in this and all subsequent references to Beadle's work.

21. Margaret Aston, *Lollards and Reformers: Images and Literacy in Late Medieval Religion* (London: Hambledon Press, 1984), 105. Aston cites an example of a crucifix corpus that viewers were invited to "read" like a "lettered parchment" (p. 104).

22. John Fuller, preface in Beadle, *Diary.*

23. Beadle, *Diary,* 7–13, 166.

24. Owen C. Watkins, *The Puritan Experience: Studies in Spiritual Autobiography* (New York: Schocken Books, 1972), 18; Beadle, *Diary,* 175.

25. Samuel Morison, ed., "The Commonplace Book of Joseph Green," *Colonial Society of Massachusetts: Transactions* 34 (1937–42): 233–34. The "Commonplace Book" contains Green's spiritual diary; his later "diary" is a more conventional journal of his ministerial career in Salem Village. See "Diary of the Rev. Joseph Green, of Salem Village," communicated by Samuel Fowler, *Historical Collections of the Essex Institute* 8 (1866): 215–24; 10 (1869): 73–104; and 36 (1900): 325–30.

26. Michael McGiffert, ed., *God's Plot: The Paradoxes of Puritan Piety, Being the Autobiography and Journal of Thomas Shepard* (Amherst: Univ. of Massachusetts Press, 1972), 181.

27. Williston Walker, *The Creeds and Platforms of Congregationalism* (Philadelphia: Pilgrim Press, 1960), 223. On the origins of the use of the relations, see Morgan, *Visible Saints,* 98–99.

28. Patricia Caldwell, *The Puritan Conversion Narrative: The Beginnings of American Expression* (Cambridge: Cambridge Univ. Press, 1983), 46.

29. Ibid., 97.

30. The history of this evolution and the development of the so-called "halfway covenant" has been investigated in numerous studies; one of the more extensive is Robert G. Pope, *The Half-Way Covenant: Church Membership in Puritan New England* (Princeton: Princeton Univ. Press, 1969).

31. Jonathan Edwards, *A Faithful Narrative of the Surprising Work of God* in *The Great Awakening,* ed. C. C. Goen, vol. 4 of *The Works of Jonathan Edwards* (New Haven: Yale Univ. Press, 1972), 176. Cf. Stephen R. Yarbrough and John C. Adams, *Delightful Conviction: Jonathan Edwards and the Rhetoric of Conversion* (Westport, Conn.: Greenwood Press, 1993), xiii.

32. Daniel B. Shea, "Jonathan Edwards: Historian of Consciousness," in *Major Writers of Early American Literature*, ed. Everett Emerson (Madison: Univ. of Wisconsin Press, 1972), 199.

33. Edwards, *Works* 4:191.

34. See for example, the analyses offered in William J. Scheick, *The Writings of Jonathan Edwards: Theme, Motif, and Style* (College Station: Texas A & M Univ. Press, 1975), 41–50; Cushing Strout, "Young People of the Awakening: The Dynamics of a Social Movement," in *Encounter with Erikson: Historical Interpretation and Religious Biography,* ed. Donald Capps et al. (Missoula, Mont.: Scholars Press, 1977), 197–98;

Yarbrough and Adams, *Delightful Conviction,* 43; and Shea, "Jonathan Edwards: Historian of Consciousness," 198.

35. Edwards, *Works* 2:162; Ola E. Winslow, *Jonathan Edwards, 1703–1758: A Biography* (New York: Macmillan, 1941), 167. See also Goen's introduction in Edwards, *Works* 4:27–30.

36. Jonathan Edwards, *Works* 4:332, 333–34. Sarah Pierpont Edwards's original account can be found in S. E. Dwight, *The Life of President Edwards* (New York, 1830), 171–86. That Edwards was consciously reacting to those who criticized the accounts of Hutchinson and Bartlet is clear in his comments about Thomas Prince's publication of Puritan Roger Clap's memoirs. The subject of that account, in Edwards's words, was not "a silly woman or child, but a man of solid understanding"; *Works* 4:312.

37. The best critical edition of Edwards's revision of Brainerd's diary is in Jonathan Edwards, *The Life of David Brainerd,* ed. Norman Pettit, *The Works of Jonathan Edwards,* vol. 7 (New Haven: Yale Univ. Press, 1985). Pettit provides in parallel columns Brainerd's original account of his conversion and the Edwardsean revision (pp. 100–153). On the influence of the work and its publishing history, see Pettit's introduction (especially pp. 3–4, 71–80); and Joseph Conforti, "Jonathan Edwards' Most Popular Work: 'The Life of David Brainerd' and Nineteenth-Century Evangelical Culture," *Church History* 54 (1985): 188–201.

38. Cf. Yarbrough and Adams, *Delightful Conviction,* 6–9. Edwards's account of his conversion was first published, in edited form, in Samuel Hopkins, *The Life and Character of the Late Reverend Mr. Jonathan Edwards* (Boston, 1765). A recent printing of the original and unedited version is in David Levin, ed., *Jonathan Edwards: A Profile* (New York: Hill and Wang, 1969), 1–86. Yarbrough and Adams argue that Edwards's conversion rhetoric failed because his traditionally Calvinistic image of the unregenerate sinner fit too closely with the "independent, self-determined individuals" that the members of his congregation were becoming; *Delightful Conviction,* xv.

39. Edwards's defense of his position on the necessity of oral relations has been recently reprinted in Jonathan Edwards, "An Humble Inquiry," in *Ecclesiastical Writings,* ed. David D. Hall, vol. 12 of *The Works of Jonathan Edwards* (New Haven: Yale Univ. Press, 1994), 167–348.

40. Lemuel Burkitt and Jesse Read, *A Concise History of the Kehukee Baptist Association* (Philadelphia, 1850; rpt., New York: Arno Press, 1980), 42.

41. Stone, *Biography,* 5.

42. Ray Potter, *Memoirs of the Life and Religious Experience of Ray Potter* (Providence, 1829), 45; Baird, *Religion in America,* 184.

43. Abner Chase, *Recollections of the Past* (New York, 1846), 14, 28; Burkitt and Read, *Concise History,* 151; David Marks, *The Life of David Marks to the 26th Year of His Age* (Limerick, Maine, 1831), 25.

44. Georges Gusdorf, "Conditions and Limits of Autobiography," in Olney, *Autobiography,* 30; Karl J. Weintraub, "Autobiography and Historical Consciousness," *Critical Inquiry* 1 (June 1975): 821.

45. Mircea Eliade, *Myths, Dreams and Mysteries: The Encounter between Contemporary Faiths and Archaic Realities,* trans. Philip Mairet (New York: Harper and Row, 1960), 14–15.

46. By neglecting to supply historical events with the "metahistorical meaning" possible through myth, Eliade argues that contemporary "modernist" societies fall victim to an arbitrary succession of meaningless events—this is what he terms "the terror of history." See Mircea Eliade, *The Myth of the Eternal Return or, Cosmos and History,* trans. Willard R. Trask (Princeton: Princeton Univ. Press, 1954), 141–62.

47. John B. Hudson, *Narrative of the Christian Experience, Travels and Labors of John B. Hudson* (Rochester, N.Y., 1838), 25; Henry Holcombe, *The First Fruits, In a Series of Letters* (Philadelphia, 1812), 29.

Chapter 3. The Paradox of the Self

1. Chase, *Recollections,* 16–17.

2. Ibid., 20, 21, 31.

3. John N. Morris, *Versions of the Self* (New York: Basic Books, 1966), 6.

4. White, *Tropics of Discourse,* 3–4.

5. Quoted in J. Neuner and J. Dupuis, *The Christian Faith in the Doctrinal Documents of the Catholic Church,* rev. ed. (New York: Alba House, 1982), 14.

6. Jaroslav Pelikan, *The Christian Tradition: A History of the Development of Doctrine,* vol. 1, *The Emergence of the Catholic Tradition (100–600)* (Chicago: Univ. of Chicago Press, 1971), 30.

7. Athanasius, "On the Incarnation of the Word," in *The Christology of the Later Fathers,* ed. Edward Rochie Hardy, Library of Christian Classics (Philadelphia: Westminster Press, 1954), 3:107; cf. Jaroslav Pelikan, *The Christian Tradition: A History of the Development of Doctrine,* vol. 2, *The Spirit of Eastern Christendom (600–1700)* (Chicago: Univ. of Chicago Press, 1974), 247.

8. Anselm, "Why God Became Man," in *A Scholastic Miscellany: Anselm to Ockham,* ed. and trans. Eugene R. Fairweather, Library of Christian Classics (Philadelphia: Westminster Press, 1956), 10:135, 151.

9. Tertullian, "The Testimony of the Soul," in *Tertullian: Apologetical Works and Minucius Felix Octavius,* trans. Rudolph Arbesmann, The Fathers of the Church: A New Translation (Washington: Catholic Univ. Press, 1950), 10:137.

10. Tertullian, "The Testimony of the Soul," 140; Gregory of Nyssa, "On the Soul and Resurrection," in *Saint Gregory of Nyssa: Ascetical Works,* trans. Virginia Woods Callahan, The Fathers of the Church: A New Translation (Washington: Catholic Univ. Press, 1967), 58:240.

11. Augustine, "The Greatness of the Soul," in *Saint Augustine: The Greatness of the Soul; The Teacher,* ed. Joseph M. Colleran, Ancient Christian Writers (New York: Newman Press, 1978), 9:110.

12. *The Confessions of St. Augustine,* trans. John K. Ryan (New York: Doubleday, 1960), 197–98.

13. My terminology suggests more precision than actually existed between these two terms. Platonism recognized a fundamental division within the human being, a "higher" and a "lower" part of the soul, that contributed to a similar war within; but this Platonic struggle was between the passions and reason. Christian theology could not accept this dichotomy because reason itself had also been corrupted by sin. See Charles Taylor, *Sources of the Self: The Making of Modern Identity* (Cambridge: Harvard Univ. Press, 1989), 115–16.

14. Walter Ullmann, *The Individual and Society in the Middle Ages* (Baltimore: Johns Hopkins Univ. Press, 1966), 7–8.

15. Ibid., 12.

16. Ibid., 116, 122. Besides feudalism and the contributions of Thomist thought, Ullmann noted the rise of the "natural" sciences, the turn to "naturalism" in art, and the increasing use of vernacular languages as indications of this new appropriation of *humanitas* during the thirteenth century.

17. Jaroslav Pelikan, *The Christian Tradition: A History of the Development of Doctrine,* vol. 4, *Reformation of Church and Dogma (1300–1700)* (Chicago: Univ. of Chicago Press, 1984), 21.

18. Taylor, *Sources of the Self,* x; Max Weber, *The Protestant Ethic and the Spirit of Capitalism* (1905; rpt., New York: Charles Scribner's Sons, 1958), 98–128.

19. John Calvin, *Institutes of the Christian Religion,* ed. John T. McNeill and trans. Ford Lewis Battles (Philadelphia: Westminster Press, 1960), 35–37, 183.

20. Thomas Shepard, *The Works of Thomas Shepard,* ed. John A. Albro (Boston, 1853; rpt., New York: AMS, 1967), 3 vols., 1:31, 2:127.

21. Thomas Hooker, *The Soules Humiliation* (London, 1640; rpt., New York: AMS Press, 1981), 145; Edwards, *Works* 2:311.

22. Peter Iver Kaufman comments on this understanding of self-knowledge as both destructive in creating a "dis-ease" of self and yet possessed of "therapeutic value" in recomposing and reconstituting the self. Kaufman, *Prayer, Despair, and Drama: Elizabethan Introspection* (Urbana and Chicago: Univ. of Illinois Press, 1996).

23. Sacvan Bercovitch, *The Puritan Origins of the American Self* (New Haven: Yale Univ. Press, 1975), 19, 22–23.

24. See Caldwell, *The Puritan Conversion Narrative,* chap. 5.

25. Charles G. Finney, *Lectures on Revivals of Religion,* (New York, 1835), 35.

26. Garrettson, *Experience,* 31; James D. Knowles, ed., *Memoir of Mrs. Ann H. Judson,* 4th ed. (Boston, 1831; rpt. New York: Garland, 1987), 19; Batchelder, *Narrative,* 31.

27. Elam Potter, *The Author's Account of His Conversion and Call to the Gospel Ministry* (Boston, 1772), 7; Asa Wild, *A Short Sketch of the Religious Experience and Spiritual Travels of Asa Wild* (Amsterdam, N.Y., 1824), 4, 13; Hosea Smith, *The Life of Hosea Smith* (Providence, 1833), 26.

28. Peter Cartwright, *Autobiography of Peter Cartwright,* ed. W. P. Strickland (New York, 1857), 27; Brereton, *From Sin to Salvation,* 17; Shea, *Spiritual Autobiography in Early America,* 106.

29. Hosea Smith, *Life,* 10.

30. Ray Potter, *Memoirs,* 14–15.

31. Nathanael Emmons, "Memoir," in *The Works of Nathanael Emmons,* ed. Jacob Idle (Boston, 1842), x–xi.

32. Garrettson, *Experience,* 9–10, 15; Elam Potter, *Author's Account,* 4, 5.

33. Theophilus Gates, *The Trials, Experience, Exercises of Mind, and First Travels of Theophilus R. Gates* (Poughkeepsie, N.Y., 1810), 64; Eleazer Sherman, *The Narrative of Eleazer Sherman* (Providence, 1832), 16.

34. Finney, *Lectures,* 16–17.

35. Garrettson, *Experience,* 30; Joseph Thomas, *The Life of the Pilgrim, Joseph Thomas* (Winchester, Va., 1817), 22.

36. Batchelder, *Narrative,* 37ff; Joshua Comstock, *A Short History of the Life of Joshua Comstock* (Providence, 1822), 5; Harriet Livermore, *A Narration of Religious Experience. In Twelve Letters* (Concord, N.H., 1826), 1:120. Although Livermore's work

was enumerated as volume 1, no subsequent volumes were published, so I have omitted the volume reference in subsequent citations.

37. Marvin S. Hill, *Quest for Refuge: The Mormon Flight from American Pluralism* (Salt Lake City: Signature Books, 1989), 14.

38. Kett, "Rural New England," 12.

39. Nathan O. Hatch, *The Democratization of American Christianity* (New Haven: Yale Univ. Press, 1989), 7; Ebersole, *Captured by Texts,* 116.

40. Ray Potter, *Memoirs,* v.

41. Henry Oliphant[?], *Memoirs and Remains of John Oliphant* (Auburn, N.Y., 1835), 9–10.

42. George Henry, *Incidents in the Life of George W. Henry* (Utica, N.Y., 1846), iv.

Chapter 4. The Language of Experience

1. Jonathan Edwards, *The Works of President Edwards,* (New York, 1829–30), 6:65; Stone, *Biography,* 202–4, 206 (emphasis in original).

2. Debora K. Shuger, *Sacred Rhetoric: The Christian Grand Style in the English Renaissance* (Princeton: Princeton Univ. Press, 1988), 109, 227.

3. Margaret Aston, *England's Iconoclasts,* vol. 1 of *Laws Against Images* (Oxford: Clarendon Press, 1988), 20.

4. John Dillenberger, *The Visual Arts and Christianity in America: The Colonial Period through the Nineteenth Century* (Chico, Calif.: Scholars Press, 1984), 14–15.

5. Paul S. Seaver, *The Puritan Lectureships: The Politics of Religious Dissent, 1560–1662* (Stanford, Calif.: Stanford Univ. Press, 1970), 40, 42; Harry S. Stout, *The New England Soul* (New York: Oxford Univ. Press, 1986), 4.

6. Miller, *The New England Mind: The Seventeenth Century* (Cambridge: Belknap Press of Harvard Univ. Press, 1954), 298; Shepard, *Works* 2:505.

7. George Selement and Bruce C. Wooley, eds., "Thomas Shepard's *Confessions,*" *Colonial Society of Massachusetts, Collections* 58 (1981): 82–84; quotation on pages 193–94. Hereafter cited as Shepard, *"Confessions."* The fifty-one oral relations collected by Shepard are the largest single group of the Puritan relations, but other collections may be found in Robert G. Pope, ed., "The Notebook of the Reverend John Fiske," *Colonial Society of Massachusetts, Collections* 47 (1974); and Michael Wigglesworth, *The Diary of Michael Wigglesworth,* ed. Edmund S. Morgan (Gloucester, Mass.: Peter Smith, 1970).

8. Darrett Rutman, *American Puritanism: Faith and Practice* (Philadelphia: J. B. Lippincott, 1970), 27.

9. Finney, *Lectures,* 164; cf. Sidney E. Mead, "The Rise of the Evangelical Conception of the Ministry in America (1607–1850)" in *The Ministry in Historical Perspectives,* ed. H. Richard Niebuhr and Daniel D. Williams (New York: Harper and Brothers, 1956), 244–49; and Loveland, *Southern Evangelicals and the Social Order,* 39.

10. Jarena Lee, *The Life and Religious Experience of Jarena Lee* (Philadelphia, 1836), 6; Cartwright, *Autobiography,* 37–38; Livermore, *Narration,* 29.

11. Sherman, *Narrative*; James Champlin, *Early Biography, Travels and Adventures of Rev. James Champlin,* 2d rev. ed. (Columbus, 1842), 102–3; Holcombe, *The First Fruits,* 26; Knowles, *Memoir of Mrs. Ann H. Judson,* 16; Hudson, *Narrative,* 25; Garrettson, *Experience,* 28.

12. Ann B. Taves, *The Household of Faith: Roman Catholic Devotions in Mid–Nineteenth-Century America* (Notre Dame, Ind.: Notre Dame Univ. Press, 1986), 4–10. Although Taves charts only the impact of these factors on the growth of Catholic devotional literature, these technological and educational advances had similar repercussions in Protestant devotionalism.

13. Charles E. Hambrick-Stowe, *The Practice of Piety: Puritan Devotional Disciplines in Seventeenth-Century New England* (Chapel Hill: Published for the Institute of Early American History and Culture by the Univ. of North Carolina Press, 1982), 157–58.

14. Elam Potter, *Author's Account,* 6–7; Garrettson, *Experience,* 17; Knowles, *Memoir of Mrs. Ann H. Judson,* 18; Devereux Jarratt, *The Life of the Reverend Devereux Jarratt* (Baltimore, 1806), 48–49.

15. Ephraim Stinchfield, *Some Memoirs of the Life, Experience, and Travels of Elder Ephraim Stinchfield* (Portland, Maine, 1819), 15; Hooper, *Life,* 5.

16. Dickson D. Bruce, *And They All Sang Hallelujah: Plain-Folk Camp-Meeting Religion, 1800–1845* (Knoxville: Univ. of Tennessee Press, 1974), 62–70; Brereton, *From Sin to Salvation,* 18.

17. Garrettson, *Experience,* v; Henry, *Incidents in the Life of George W. Henry,* iii.

18. Brereton, *From Sin to Salvation,* 16.

19. Ray Potter, *Memoirs,* 45.

20. My argument here generally follows that of Peter G. Stromberg in *Language and Self-Transformation.*

21. Abner Jones, *Memoirs of the Life and Experience, Travels and Preaching of Abner Jones* (Exeter, N.H., 1807), 15.

22. Sherman, *Narrative,* 13.

23. Chase, *Recollections,* 20; Gates, *Trials,* 62.

24. Stromberg, *Language and Self-Transformation,* 6.

25. Susan F. Harding, "Convicted by the Holy Spirit: The Rhetoric of Fundamental-ist Baptist Conversion," *American Ethnologist* 14 (1987): 167–69; quotation from page 167 (emphasis in the original).
26. Holcombe, *The First Fruits,* 15.
27. Chase, *Recollections,* 16–17.
28. Fish, *Is There a Text in This Class?,* 13.
29. Shepard, *"Confessions,"* 118, 141. It is not clear whether Brewer was extended church membership, but proffer of such was highly likely despite her liabilities.
30. Ray Potter, *Memoirs,* 45; Baird Tipson, "Invisible Saints: The 'Judgment of Char-ity' in the Early New England Churches," *Church History* 44 (1975): 460–71.

Chapter 5. The Language of the Sacred

1. Bronislaw Malinowski, *Magic, Science and Religion and Other Essays* (Garden City, N.Y.: Doubleday, 1954), 29–31. See also Stromberg, *Language and Self-Transformation,* 120.
2. Stromberg, *Language and Self-Transformation,* 120 (emphasis mine). Stromberg bor-rows the term "canonical language" from Roy A. Rappaport, "Obvious Aspects of Ritual," in *Ecology, Meaning, and Religion* (Richmond, Calif.: North Atlantic Books, 1979), 173–221. For Rappaport, the "canonical language" of ritual concerns "endur-ing aspects of nature, society, or cosmos," while "indexical language" has to do with "the current status of the participants" (p. 182). While canonical language is thus "in-variant" to a large extent, it is nonetheless crucial because it is the language that actu-alizes ritual transformation. Borrowing himself from the philosopher J. L. Austin, Rappaport terms such canonical language "performative"; see J. L. Austin, *Philosophi-cal Papers,* ed. J. O. Urmson and G. J. Warnock, 2d ed. (Oxford: Clarendon Press, 1970), 233–52.
3. Ray Potter, *Memoirs,* 45.
4. Mircea Eliade, *The Sacred and the Profane: The Nature of Religion,* trans. Willard R. Trask (New York: Harcourt Brace Jovanovich, 1959), chap. 1–2; quotes from pages 72, 20–21. See also Ronald L. Grimes, *Beginnings in Ritual Studies* (Lanham, Md.: Univ. Press of America, 1982), 55, who prefers the phrases "crucial times" and "founded places."
5. Charles G. Finney, *An Autobiography* (Old Tappan, N.J.: Fleming H. Revell, 1876), 14.
6. Calvin Colton, *History and Character of American Revivals of Religion* (London, 1832; rpt., New York: AMS Press, 1973), 212.

7. Henry, *Incidents in the Life of George W. Henry,* 255.

8. Hudson, *Narrative,* 34; Ariel Kendrick, *Sketches of the Life and Times of Eld. Ariel Kendrick* (Ludlow, Vt., 1847), 15; Elias Smith, *Life,* 67, 59; Ray Potter, *Memoirs,* 25.

9. Peter Howell, *The Life and Travels of Peter Howell* (New Bern, N.C., 1849), 7; Comstock, *Short History,* 6; Thomas, *Life,* 22; Hudson, *Narrative,* 35.

10. Chase, *Recollections,* 21; Garrettson, *Experience,* 27, 30; Elam Potter, *Author's Account,* 15.

11. Wigglesworth, *Diary,* 110; Shepard, *"Confessions,"* 191, 128.

12. Ray Potter, *Memoirs,* 26.

13. Knowles, *Memoir of Mrs. Ann H. Judson,* 16 (emphasis in original); Livermore, *Narration,* 57; Elam Potter, *Author's Account,* 6, 12; Garrettson, *Experience,* 28–29.

14. Solomon Mack, *A Narraitve [sic] of the Life of Solomon Mack* (Windsor, Conn., [1811]), 24–25; Hosea Smith, *Life,* 14; Jarena Lee, *Life,* 8. As the title of Mack's autobiography is an obvious misprint, I have not repeated this error in subsequent references.

15. Stephen H. Bradley, *A Sketch of the Life of Stephen H. Bradley* (Madison, Conn., 1830), 3.

16. Wild, *Short Sketch,* 4.

17. Howell, *Life,* 6; Elam Potter, *Author's Account,* 14.

18. Levi Hathaway, *The Narrative of Levi Hathaway* (Providence, 1820), 32

19. Howell, *Life,* 2–6, quotation from page 2; Ray Potter, *Memoirs,* 27; Billy Hibbard, *Memoirs of the Life and Travels of B. Hibbard,* 2d ed. (New York, 1843), 24.

20. Elam Potter, *Author's Account,* 9; J. W. Holman, "A Sketch of the Life, Experience, and Travels of the Author," in *The Faith Once Delivered to the Saints* (Philadelphia, 1830), 63.

21. Mack, *Narrative,* 18, 21. Mack estimated his age at seventy-six, but Richard Lloyd Anderson has argued convincingly that Mack was at least two years older than he believed himself to be; Anderson, *Joseph Smith's New England Heritage: Influences of Grandfathers Solomon Mack and Asael Smith* (Salt Lake City: Deseret Book Co., 1971), 162n.

22. Mack, *Narrative,* 22–25; quotation from page 22.

23. Perry Miller, *The New England Mind: From Colony to Province* (Cambridge: Belknap Press of Harvard Univ. Press, 1953), chap. 8; and "From the Covenant to the Revival," in *The Shaping of American Religion,* eds. James Ward Smith and A. Leland Jamison, vol. 1 of *Religion in American Life* (Princeton: Princeton Univ. Press, 1961), 322–68; Leigh Eric Schmidt, *Holy Fairs: Scottish Communions and American Revivals in the Early Modern Period* (Princeton: Princeton Univ. Press, 1989).

24. Marilyn J. Westerkamp, *Triumph of the Laity: Scots-Irish Piety and the Great Awakening, 1625–1760* (New York: Oxford Univ. Press, 1988), 28; Susan O'Brien, "The Great Awakening and the First Evangelical Network," *American Historical Review* 91 (1986): 811–32.

25. Bruce, *And They All Sang Hallelujah,* 71–73. Charles A. Johnson credited the frontier revivals with originating this practice; see Johnson, *The Frontier Camp Meeting: Religion's Harvest Time* (Dallas: Southern Methodist Univ. Press, 1955), 132–33.

26. Colton, *History and Character,* 95–96.

27. Finney, *Autobiography,* 289. On the claims of origination, see Nathan Bangs, *A History of the Methodist Episcopal Church,* 3d ed. (New York, 1840–53), 3:375; and Burkitt and Read, *Concise History,* 149.

28. Victor Turner, *The Ritual Process: Structure and Anti-Structure* (Ithaca: Cornell Univ. Press, 1969), 94–95. Cf. Arnold Van Gennep, *The Rites of Passage,* trans. Monika B. Vizedom and Gabrielle L. Caffee (1909; rpt., Chicago: Univ. of Chicago Press, 1960).

29. Howell, *Life and Travels,* 6–7; Cartwright, *Autobiography,* 37–38; John Peak, *Memoir of Elder John Peak,* 2d ed. (Boston, 1832), 30.

30. Marks, *Life,* 24; Livermore, *Narration,* 29; Ray Potter, *Memoirs,* 28.

31. Mack, *Narrative,* 4.

32. Hooper, *Life,* 3.

33. Elbert Osborn, *Passages in the Life and Ministry of Elbert Osborn* (New York, 1847–50), 1:18–19; Garrettson, *Experience,* 17; Hudson, *Narrative,* 34.

34. Elam Potter, *Author's Account,* 7–9; Comstock, *Short History,* 5; Peak, *Memoir,* 27–30.

35. Champlin, *Early Biography,* 104; Giles, *Pioneer,* 34.

36. Jones, *Memoirs,* 7 (ellipsis in original); Holcombe, *The First Fruits,* 28; Chase, *Recollections,* 18.

37. Ray Potter, *Memoirs,* 26, 30; Marks, *Life,* 20.

38. Elaw, *Memoirs,* 6; Knowles, *Memoir of Mrs. Ann Judson,* 18; Livermore, *Narration,* 48.

39. Richard Lee, *A Short Narrative of the Life of Mr. Richard Lee* (Kennebunk, Maine, 1804), 8; Hooper, *Life,* 5.

40. Marks, *Life,* 20; Hibbard, *Memoirs,* 23, 25; Holman, "Sketch," 64.

41. Nathan Noyes, *A Short Account of the Life and Experience of Nathan Noyes* (Detroit, 1847), 7; Garrettson, *Experience,* 30; Ray Potter, *Memoirs,* 27; Champlin, *Early Biography,* 104–5.

42. Stone, *Biography*, 5; Hosea Smith, *Life*, 27; Noyes, *Short Account*, 9; Elaw, *Memoirs*, 5–6.

43. Bradley, *Sketch*, 3; Ray Potter, *Memoirs*, 25; William Keith, *The Experience of William Keith* (Utica, 1806), 7.

44. Hibbard, *Memoirs*, 24–26.

45. Giles, *Pioneer*, 73.

46. Victor Turner, *The Ritual Process*, 94–97.

47. Sherman, *Narrative*, 16; Knowles, *Memoir of Mrs. Ann Judson*, 20.

48. Bradley, *Sketch*, 3.

49. Hudson, *Narrative*, 34; Chase, *Recollections*, 21; Hosea Smith, *Life*, 12.

50. Rodger M. Payne, "Metaphors of the Self and the Sacred: The Spiritual Autobiography of the Rev. Freeborn Garrettson," *Early American Literature* 27 (1992): 38–43.

51. Gates, *Trials*, 62–63.

52. William G. McLoughlin, *Revivals, Awakenings, and Reform: An Essay on Religious and Social Change in America, 1607–1977* (Chicago: Univ. of Chicago Press), 10.

Conclusion

1. Stromberg, *Language and Self-Transformation*, 6.

2. James Ireland, *The Life of the Rev. James Ireland* (Winchester, Va., 1819), 7. To avoid burdening this chapter with excessive notes, I have cited all subsequent references to this work parenthetically in the text.

3. Caldwell, *The Puritan Conversion Narrative*, 119–34.

4. Biographical vignettes of Ireland can be found in William Fristoe, *A Concise History of the Ketocton Baptist Association* (Staunton, Va., 1808), 146–48; James B. Taylor, *Virginia Baptist Ministers*, Series I (Philadelphia, 1859), 115–26; and Garnett Ryland, *The Baptists of Virginia, 1699–1926* (Richmond: Virginia Baptist Board of Missions and Education, 1955), 47–49. All of these works draw heavily and uncritically from Ireland's autobiography.

BIBLIOGRAPHY

Primary Sources

Anselm, Saint. "Why God Became Man." In *A Scholastic Miscellany: Anselm to Ockham,* ed. and trans. Eugene R. Fairweather. Vol. 10. Library of Christian Classics. Philadelphia: Westminster Press, 1956.

Athanasius, Saint. "On the Incarnation of the Word." In *The Christology of the Later Fathers,* ed. Edward Rochie Hardy. Vol. 3. Library of Christian Classics. Philadelphia: Westminster Press, 1954.

Augustine, Saint. "The Greatness of the Soul." In *Saint Augustine: The Greatness of the Soul; The Teacher,* ed. Joseph M. Colleran. Vol. 9. Ancient Christian Writers. New York: Newman Press, 1978.

————. *The Confessions of St. Augustine.* Trans. John K. Ryan. New York: Doubleday, 1960.

Bangs, Nathan. *A History of the Methodist Episcopal Church.* 3d ed. 4 vols. New York, 1840–53.

Batchelder, George W. *A Narrative of the Life, Travels and Religious Experience, of George W. Batchelder.* Philadelphia, 1843.

B[eadle], J[ohn]. *The Journal or Diary of a Thankful Christian, Presented in Some Meditations upon Numb. 33.2.* London, 1652.

Bradley, Stephen H. *A Sketch of the Life of Stephen H. Bradley.* Madison, Conn., 1830.

Burkitt, Lemuel, and Jesse Read. *A Concise History of the Kehukee Baptist Association.* Philadelphia, 1850. Rpt. New York: Arno Press, 1980.

Calvin, John. *Institutes of the Christian Religion.* 2 vols. Ed. John T. McNeill and trans. Ford Lewis Battles. Philadelphia: Westminster Press, 1960.

Cartwright, Peter. *Autobiography of Peter Cartwright.* Ed. W. P. Strickland. New York, 1857.

Champlin, James. *Early Biography, Travels and Adventures of Rev. James Champlin.* 2d rev. ed. Columbus, 1842.

Chase, Abner. *Recollections of the Past.* New York, 1846.

Colton, Calvin. *History and Character of American Revivals of Religion.* London, 1832. Rpt. New York: AMS Press, 1973.

Comstock, Joshua. *A Short History of the Life of Joshua Comstock.* Providence, 1822.

Dwight, S. E. *The Life of President Edwards.* New York, 1830.

Edwards, Jonathan. *The Works of Jonathan Edwards.* 13 vols. to date. New Haven: Yale Univ. Press, 1957–.

———. *The Works of President Edwards.* 10 vols. New York, 1830.

Elaw, Zilpha. *Memoirs of the Life, Religious Experience, Ministerial Travels and Labours of Mrs. Zilpha Elaw.* London, 1846.

Emmons, Nathanael. "Memoir." In *The Works of Nathanael Emmons,* ix–xxxvii. Boston, 1842,.

Finney, Charles G. *An Autobiography.* Old Tappan, N.J., 1876.

———. *Lectures on Revivals of Religion.* New York, 1835.

Fristoe, William. *A Concise History of the Ketocton Baptist Association.* Staunton, Va., 1808.

Garrettson, Freeborn. *The Experience and Travels of Mr. Freeborn Garrettson.* Philadelphia, 1791.

Gates, Theophilus. *The Trials, Experience, Exercises of Mind, and First Travels of Theophilus R. Gates.* Poughkeepsie, N.Y., 1810.

Giles, Charles. *Pioneer: A Narrative of the Nativity, Experience, Travels, and Ministerial Labours of Rev. Charles Giles.* New York, 1844.

Gregory of Nyssa. "On the Soul and Resurrection." In *Saint Gregory of Nyssa: Ascetical Works,* trans. Virginia Woods Callahan. Vol. 58. The Fathers of the Church: A New Translation. Washington: Catholic Univ. Press, 1967.

Hathaway, Levi. *The Narrative of Levi Hathaway.* Providence, 1820.

Henry, George. *Incidents in the Life of George W. Henry.* Utica, N.Y., 1846.

Hibbard, Billy. *Memoirs of the Life and Travels of B. Hibbard.* 2d ed. New York, 1843.

Holcombe, Henry. *The First Fruits, In a Series of Letters.* Philadelphia, 1812.

Holman, J. W. "A Sketch of the Life, Experience, and Travels of the Author." In *The Faith Once Delivered to the Saints,* 58–85. Philadelphia, 1830.

Hooker, Thomas. *The Soules Humiliation.* London, 1640. Rpt. New York: AMS Press, 1981.

Hooper, James. *Life and Sentiments of James Hooper.* Paris, Maine, 1834.

Hopkins, Samuel. *The Life and Character of the Late Reverend Mr. Jonathan Edwards.* Boston, 1765.

Howell, Peter. *The Life and Travels of Peter Howell.* New Bern, N.C., 1849.

Hudson, John B. *Narrative of the Christian Experience, Travels and Labors of John B. Hudson.* Rochester, N.Y., 1838.

Ireland, James. *The Life of the Rev. James Ireland.* Winchester, Va., 1819.

Jarratt, Devereux. *The Life of the Reverend Devereux Jarratt.* Baltimore, 1806.

Jones, Abner. *Memoirs of the Life and Experience, Travels and Preaching of Abner Jones.* Exeter, N.H., 1807.

Knowles, James D., ed. *Memoir of Mrs. Ann H. Judson.* 4th ed. Boston, 1831. Rpt. New York: Garland, 1987.

Keith, William Keith. *The Experience of William Keith.* Utica, 1806.

Kendrick, Ariel. *Sketches of the Life and Times of Eld. Ariel Kendrick.* Ludlow, Vt., 1847.

Lee, Jarena. *The Life and Religious Experience of Jarena Lee.* Philadelphia, 1836.

Lee, Richard. *A Short Narrative of the Life of Mr. Richard Lee.* Kennebunk, Maine, 1804.

Livermore, Harriet. *A Narration of Religious Experience.* Concord, N.H., 1826.

Mack, Solomon. *A Narraitve [sic] of the Life of Solomon Mack.* Windsor, Conn., [1811].

Marks, David. *The Life of David Marks to the 26th Year of His Age.* Limerick, Maine, 1831.

McGiffert, Michael, ed. *God's Plot: The Paradoxes of Puritan Piety, Being the Autobiography and Journal of Thomas Shepard.* Amherst: Univ. of Massachusetts Press, 1972.

Morison, Samuel, ed. "The Commonplace Book of Joseph Green." *Colonial Society of Massachusetts: Transactions* 34 (1937–42): 233–34.

Neuner, J., and J. Dupuis. *The Christian Faith in the Doctrinal Documents of the Catholic Church.* Rev. ed. New York: Alba House, 1982.

Noyes, Nathan. *A Short Account of the Life and Experience of Nathan Noyes.* Detroit, 1847.

Oliphant, Henry[?]. *Memoirs and Remains of John Oliphant.* Auburn, N.Y., 1835.

Osborn, Elbert. *Passages in the Life and Ministry of Elbert Osborn.* 2 vols. New York, 1847–50.

Peak, John. *Memoir of Elder John Peak.* 2d ed. Boston, 1832.

Pope, Robert G., ed. "The Notebook of the Reverend John Fiske." *Colonial Society of Massachusetts, Collections* 47 (1974).

Potter, Elam. *The Author's Account of His Conversion and Call to the Gospel Ministry.* Boston, 1772.

Potter, Ray. *Memoirs of the Life and Religious Experience of Ray Potter.* Providence, 1829.

Selement, George C., and Bruce C. Wooley, eds. "Thomas Shepard's *Confessions.*" *Colonial Society of Massachusetts, Collections* 58 (1981).

Shepard, Thomas. *The Works of Thomas Shepard.* 3 vols. Ed. John A. Albro. Boston, 1853. Rpt. New York: AMS, 1967.

Sherman, Eleazer. *The Narrative of Eleazer Sherman.* Providence, 1832.

Smith, Elias. *The Life, Conversion, Preaching, Travels, and Sufferings of Elias Smith.* Portsmouth, N.H., 1816.

Smith, Hosea. *The Life of Hosea Smith.* Providence, 1833.

Stinchfield, Ephraim. *Some Memoirs of the Life, Experience, and Travels of Elder Ephraim Stinchfield.* Portland, Maine, 1819.

Stone, Barton Warren. *The Biography of Eld. Barton Warren Stone, Written by Himself: With Additions and Reflections by Elder John Rogers.* Cincinnati, 1847.

Taylor, James B. *Virginia Baptist Ministers.* Series I. Philadelphia, 1859.

Tertullian. "The Testimony of the Soul." In *Tertullian: Apologetical Works and Minucius Felix Octavius,* trans. Rudolph Arbesmann. Vol. 10. The Fathers of the Church: A New Translation. Washington, D.C.: Catholic Univ. Press, 1950.

Thomas, Joseph. *The Life of the Pilgrim, Joseph Thomas.* Winchester, Va., 1817.

Towle, Nancy. *Vicissitudes Illustrated, in the Experience of Nancy Towle.* 2d ed. Portsmouth, N.H., 1833.

Wigglesworth, Michael. *The Diary of Michael Wigglesworth.* Ed. Edmund S. Morgan. Gloucester, Mass.: Peter Smith, 1970.

Wild, Asa. *A Short Sketch of the Religious Experience and Spiritual Travels of Asa Wild.* Amsterdam, N.Y., 1824.

Secondary Works

Ahlstrom, Sydney E. *A Religious History of the American People.* 2 vols. Garden City, N.Y.: Image Books, 1975.

Anderson, Richard Lloyd. *Joseph Smith's New England Heritage: Influences of Grandfathers Solomon Mack and Asael Smith.* Salt Lake City: Deseret Book Co., 1971.

Andrews, William L. *To Tell a Free Story: The First Century of Afro-American Autobiography, 1760–1865.* Urbana and Chicago: Univ. of Illinois Press, 1986.

Aston, Margaret. *England's Iconoclasts.* Vol. 1. *Laws Against Images.* Oxford: Clarendon Press, 1988.

————. *Lollards and Reformers: Images and Literacy in Late Medieval Religion.* London: Hambledon Press, 1984.

Aubin, Paul. *Le problème de la "conversion": Étude sur un term commun a l'Hellénisme et au Christianisme des trois premiers siècles.* Paris: Beauchesne et ses Fils, 1963.

Austin, J. L. *Philosophical Papers.* 2d ed. Ed. J. O. Urmson and G. J. Warnock. Oxford: Clarendon Press, 1970.

Baird, Robert. *Religion in America; or, An Account of the Origin, Progress, Relation to the State, and Present Condition of the Evangelical Churches in the United States. With Notices of the Unevangelical Denominations.* New York, 1844.

Balmer, Randall. "Eschewing the 'Routine of Religion': Eighteenth–Century Pietism and the Revival Tradition in America." In *Modern Christian Revivals,* ed. Edith L. Blumhofer and Randall Balmer, 1–16. Urbana and Chicago: Univ. of Illinois Press, 1993.

Bercovitch, Sacvan. *The Puritan Origins of the American Self.* New Haven: Yale Univ. Press, 1975.

Boles, John B. *The Great Revival, 1787–1805.* Lexington: Univ. Press of Kentucky, 1972.

Brauer, Jerald C. "Conversion: From Puritanism to Revivalism." *Journal of Religion* 58 (1978): 227–43.

Breitenbach, William. "The Consistent Calvinism of the New Divinity Movement." *William and Mary Quarterly,* 3d ser., 41 (1984): 241–64.

Brereton, Virginia Lieson. *From Sin to Salvation: Stories of Women's Conversions, 1800 to the Present.* Bloomington: Indiana Univ. Press, 1991.

Bruce, Dickson D. *And They All Sang Hallelujah: Plain-Folk Camp-Meeting Religion, 1800–1845.* Knoxville: Univ. of Tennessee Press, 1974.

Bruss, Elizabeth W. *Autobiographical Acts: The Changing Situation of a Literary Genre.* Baltimore: Johns Hopkins Univ. Press, 1976.

Buckley, Jerome Hamilton. *The Turning Key: Autobiography and the Subjective Impulse since 1800.* Cambridge: Harvard Univ. Press, 1984.

Caldwell, Patricia. *The Puritan Conversion Narrative: The Beginnings of American Expression.* Cambridge: Cambridge Univ. Press, 1983.

Campbell, Ted A. *The Religion of the Heart: A Study of European Religious Life in the Seventeenth and Eighteenth Centuries.* Columbia: Univ. of South Carolina Press, 1991.

Cohen, Daniel A. *Pillars of Salt, Monuments of Grace: New England Crime Literature and the Origins of American Popular Culture, 1674–1860.* New York: Oxford Univ. Press, 1993.

Conforti, Joseph. "Jonathan Edwards' Most Popular Work: 'The Life of David Brainerd' and Nineteenth-Century Evangelical Culture." *Church History* 54 (1985): 188–201.

———. *Samuel Hopkins and the New Divinity Movement: Calvinism, the Congregational Ministry, and Reform in New England Between the Great Awakenings.* Grand Rapids: Christian Univ. Press, 1981.

Courcelle, Pierre. *Les Confessions de saint Augustine dans le tradition littéraire: Antécédents et postérité.* Paris: Études Augustiniennes, 1963.

Cox, Patricia. *Biography in Late Antiquity: A Quest for the Holy Man.* Berkeley and Los Angeles: Univ. of California Press, 1983.

Dillenberger, John. *The Visual Arts and Christianity in America: The Colonial Period through the Nineteenth Century.* Chico, Calif.: Scholars Press, 1984.

Dilthey, Wilhelm. *Pattern and Meaning in History: Thoughts on History and Society.* Ed. H. P. Rickman. New York: Harper, 1961.

Dorsey, Peter A. *Sacred Estrangement: The Rhetoric of Conversion in Modern American Autobiography.* University Park: Pennsylvania State Univ. Press, 1993.

Ebersole, Gary L. *Captured by Texts: Puritan to Postmodern Images of Indian Captivity.* Charlottesville and London: Univ. Press of Virginia, 1995.

Eliade, Mircea. *Myths, Dreams and Mysteries: The Encounter between Contemporary Faiths and Archaic Realities.* Trans. Philip Mairet. New York: Harper and Row, 1960.

———. *The Sacred and the Profane: The Nature of Religion.* Trans. Willard R. Trask. New York: Harcourt Brace Jovanovich, 1959.

———. *The Myth of the Eternal Return or, Cosmos and History.* Trans. Willard R. Trask. Princeton: Princeton Univ. Press, 1954.

Fish, Stanley. *Is There a Text in This Class? The Authority of Interpretive Communities.* Cambridge: Harvard Univ. Press, 1980.

Foucault, Michel. "What Is an Author?" In *Textual Strategies: Perspectives in Post-Structuralist Criticism,* ed. Josué V. Harari, 141–60. Ithaca: Cornell Univ. Press, 1979.

———. *The Birth of the Clinic: An Archaeology of Medical Perception.* Trans. A. M. Sheridan-Smith. New York: Vintage, 1973.

———. *The Archaeology of Knowledge.* Trans. A. M. Sheridan-Smith. New York: Pantheon, 1972.

———. *Madness and Civilization: A History of Insanity in the Age of Reason.* Trans. Richard Howard. New York: Pantheon, 1965.

Gaventa, Beverly Roberts. *From Darkness to Light: Aspects of Conversion in the New Testament.* Philadelphia: Fortress Press, 1986.

Geertz, Clifford. *The Interpretation of Cultures.* New York: Basic Books, 1973.

Goodenough, Edwin. *The Theology of Justin Martyr: An Investigation into the Conceptions of Early Christian Literature and Its Hellenistic and Judaistic Influences.* Jena, 1923. Rpt. Amsterdam: Philo Press, 1968.

Greenblatt, Stephen. *Renaissance Self-Fashioning: From More to Shakespeare.* Chicago: Univ. of Chicago Press, 1980.

Grimes, Ronald L. *Beginnings in Ritual Studies.* Lanham, Md.: Univ. Press of America, 1982.

Haller, William. *The Rise of Puritanism.* New York: Columbia Univ. Press, 1938.

Hambrick-Stowe, Charles E. *The Practice of Piety: Puritan Devotional Disciplines in Seventeenth-Century New England.* Chapel Hill: Published for the Institute of Early American History and Culture by the Univ. of North Carolina Press, 1982.

Harding, Susan F. "Convicted by the Holy Spirit: The Rhetoric of Fundamentalist Baptist Conversion." *American Ethnologist* 14 (1987): 167–81.

Harran, Marilyn J. *Luther on Conversion: The Early Years.* Ithaca: Cornell Univ. Press, 1983.

Hatch, Nathan O. *The Democratization of American Christianity.* New Haven: Yale Univ. Press, 1989.

Hefferman, Thomas J. *Sacred Biography: Saints and Their Biographers in the Middle Ages.* New York: Oxford, 1988.

Hill, Marvin S. Hill. *Quest for Refuge: The Mormon Flight from American Pluralism.* Salt Lake City: Signature Books, 1989.

Holladay, William L. *The Root Sûbh in the Old Testament.* Leiden: E. J. Brill, 1958.

Hunter, James Davison. *American Evangelicalism: Conservative Religion and the Quandary of Modernity.* New Brunswick, N.J.: Rutgers Univ. Press, 1983.

James, William. *The Varieties of Religious Experience.* 1902. Rpt. New York: Penguin, 1982.

Johnson, Charles A. *The Frontier Camp Meeting: Religion's Harvest Time.* Dallas: Southern Methodist Univ. Press, 1955.

Kaufman, Peter Iver. *Prayer, Despair, and Drama: Elizabethan Introspection.* Urbana and Chicago: Univ. of Illinois Press, 1996.

Kett, Joseph F. "Growing Up in Rural New England, 1800–1840." In *Anonymous Americans: Explorations in Nineteenth-Century Social History,* ed. Tamara K. Hareven, 1–16. Englewood Cliffs, N.J.: Prentice-Hall, 1971.

Lehmann, Paul. "Autobiography in the Middle Ages." *Transactions of the Royal Historical Society,* 5th ser., 3 (1953): 41–52.

Levin, David, ed. *Jonathan Edwards: A Profile*. New York: Hill and Wang, 1969.

Loveland, Anne C. *Southern Evangelicals and the Social Order, 1800–1860*. Baton Rouge: Louisiana State Univ. Press, 1980.

Lyons, George. *Pauline Autobiography: Toward a New Understanding*. Vol. 73. Society of Biblical Literature Dissertation Series. Atlanta: Scholars Press, 1985.

Lyons, John O. *The Invention of the Self: The Hinge of Consciousness in the Eighteenth Century*. Carbondale: Southern Illinois Univ. Press, 1978.

Malinowski, Bronislaw. *Magic, Science and Religion and Other Essays*. Garden City, N.Y.: Doubleday, 1954.

Marsden, George M. *Understanding Fundamentalism and Evangelicalism*. Grand Rapids: William B. Eerdmans, 1991.

McLoughlin, William G. *The American Evangelicals, 1800–1900: An Anthology*. Gloucester, Mass.: Peter Smith, 1976.

———. *Revivals, Awakenings, and Reform: An Essay on Religious and Social Change in America, 1607–1977*. Chicago: Univ. of Chicago Press, 1978.

Mead, Sidney E. Mead. "The Rise of the Evangelical Conception of the Ministry in America (1607–1850)." In *The Ministry in Historical Perspectives*, ed. H. Richard Niebuhr and Daniel D. Williams, 207–49. New York: Harper and Brothers, 1956.

———. *Nathaniel William Taylor, 1786–1858: A Connecticut Liberal*. Chicago: Univ. of Chicago Press, 1942.

Miller, Perry. "From the Covenant to the Revival." In *The Shaping of American Religion*, ed. James Ward Smith and A. Leland Jamison, 322–68. Vol. 1. *Religion in American Life*. Princeton: Princeton Univ. Press, 1961.

———. *The New England Mind: The Seventeenth Century*. Cambridge: Belknap Press of Harvard Univ. Press, 1954.

———. *The New England Mind: From Colony to Province*. Cambridge: Belknap Press of Harvard Univ. Press, 1953.

Morgan, Edmund S. *Visible Saints: The History of a Puritan Idea*. Ithaca: Cornell Univ. Press, 1963.

Morris, John N. *Versions of the Self*. New York: Basic Books, 1966.

Morrison, Karl F. *Understanding Conversion*. Charlottesville and London: Univ. Press of Virginia, 1992.

Musurillo, Herbert. *The Acts of the Christian Martyrs*. Oxford: Clarendon Press, 1972.

Nock, A. D. *Conversion: The Old and the New in Religion from Alexander the Great to Augustine of Hippo*. London: Oxford Univ. Press, 1961.

O'Brien, Susan. "The Great Awakening and the First Evangelical Network." *American Historical Review* 91 (1986): 811–32.

Olney, James, ed. *Autobiography: Essays Theoretical and Critical.* Princeton: Princeton Univ. Press, 1980.

Ozment, Steven. *The Age of Reform, 1250–1550: An Intellectual and Religious History of Late Medieval and Reformation Europe.* New Haven: Yale Univ. Press, 1980.

Payne, Rodger M. "Metaphors of the Self and the Sacred: The Spiritual Autobiography of the Rev. Freeborn Garrettson." *Early American Literature* 27 (1992): 31–48.

Pelikan, Jaroslav. *The Christian Tradition: A History of the Development of Doctrine.* 5 vols. Chicago: Univ. of Chicago Press, 1971–89.

Pope, Robert G. *The Half-Way Covenant: Church Membership in Puritan New England.* Princeton: Princeton Univ. Press, 1969.

Rambo, Lewis R. *Understanding Religious Conversion.* New Haven: Yale Univ. Press, 1993.

Rappaport, Roy A. "Obvious Aspects of Ritual." In *Ecology, Meaning, and Religion,* 173–221. Richmond, Calif.: North Atlantic Books, 1979.

Rutman, Darrett. *American Puritanism: Faith and Practice.* Philadelphia: J. B. Lippincott, 1970.

Ryland, Garnett. *The Baptists of Virginia, 1699–1926.* Richmond: Virginia Baptist Board of Missions and Education, 1955.

Sayre, Robert F. "Religious Autobiography." In *Encyclopedia of the American Religious Experience: Studies of Traditions and Movements,* ed. Charles H. Lippy and Peter W. Williams. 3 vols. New York: Charles Scribner's Sons, 1988.

Scheick, William J. *The Writings of Jonathan Edwards: Theme, Motif, and Style.* College Station: Texas A & M Univ. Press, 1975.

Schmidt, Leigh Eric. *Holy Fairs: Scottish Communions and American Revivals in the Early Modern Period.* Princeton: Princeton Univ. Press, 1989.

Seaver, Paul S. *The Puritan Lectureships: The Politics of Religious Dissent, 1560–1662.* Stanford, Calif.: Stanford Univ. Press, 1970.

Shea, Daniel B. "Jonathan Edwards: Historian of Consciousness." In *Major Writers of Early American Literature,* ed. Everett Emerson, 179–204. Madison: Univ. of Wisconsin Press, 1972.

———. *Spiritual Autobiography in Early America.* Princeton: Princeton Univ. Press, 1968.

Shuger, Debora K. *Sacred Rhetoric: The Christian Grand Style in the English Renaissance.* Princeton: Princeton Univ. Press, 1988.

Starbuck, Edwin Diller. *The Psychology of Religion: An Empirical Study of the Growth of Religious Consciousness.* London, 1899. Rpt. New York: Charles Scribner's Sons, 1908.

Stendahl, Krister. *Paul Among Jews and Gentiles and Other Essays.* Philadelphia: Fortress Press, 1976.

Stoeffler, F. Ernest. *Rise of Evangelical Pietism.* Leiden: E. J. Brill, 1965.

Stout, Harry S. *The New England Soul.* New York: Oxford Univ. Press, 1986.

Stromberg, Peter G. *Language and Self-Transformation: A Study of the Christian Conversion Narrative.* New York: Cambridge Univ. Press, 1993.

Strout, Cushing. "Young People of the Awakening: The Dynamics of a Social Movement." In *Encounter with Erikson: Historical Interpretation and Religious Biography,* ed. Donald Capps et al., 183–216. Missoula, Mont.: Scholars Press, 1977.

Taves, Ann B. *The Household of Faith: Roman Catholic Devotions in Mid-Nineteenth-Century America.* Notre Dame, Ind.: Notre Dame Univ. Press, 1986.

Taylor, Charles. *Sources of the Self: The Making of Modern Identity.* Cambridge: Harvard Univ. Press, 1989.

Tipson, Baird. "Invisible Saints: The 'Judgment of Charity' in the Early New England Churches." *Church History* 44 (1975): 460–71.

Turner, Victor. *The Ritual Process: Structure and Anti-Structure.* Ithaca: Cornell Univ. Press, 1969.

Ullmann, Walter. *The Individual and Society in the Middle Ages.* Baltimore: Johns Hopkins Univ. Press, 1966.

Van der Leeuw, G. *Religion in Essence and Manifestation.* 2 vols. Gloucester, Mass.: Peter Smith, 1967.

Van Gennep, Arnold. *The Rites of Passage.* Trans. Monika B. Vizedom and Gabrielle L. Caffee. 1909. Rpt. Chicago: Univ. of Chicago Press, 1960.

Vaughan, Alden T., and Edward W. Clark. *Puritans Among the Indians: Accounts of Captivity and Redemption.* Cambridge: Belknap Press of the Harvard Univ. Press, 1981.

Walker, Williston. *The Creeds and Platforms of Congregationalism.* Philadelphia: Pilgrim Press, 1960.

Watkins, Owen C. *The Puritan Experience: Studies in Spiritual Autobiography.* New York: Schocken Books, 1972.

Webber, Joan. *The Eloquent "I": Style and Self in Seventeenth-Century Prose.* Madison: Univ. of Wisconsin Press, 1968.

Weber, Max. *The Protestant Ethic and the Spirit of Capitalism.* New York: Charles Scribner's Sons, 1958.

Weber, Timothy P. "Premillennialism and the Branches of Evangelicalism." In *The Variety of American Evangelicalism,* ed. Donald W. Dayton and Robert K. Johnson, 5–21. Knoxville: Univ. of Tennessee Press, 1991.

Weintraub, Karl J. *The Value of the Individual: Self and Circumstance in Autobiography.* Chicago: Univ. of Chicago Press, 1978.

———. "Autobiography and Historical Consciousness." *Critical Inquiry* 1 (June 1975): 821–48.

Westerkamp, Marilyn J. *Triumph of the Laity: Scots-Irish Piety and the Great Awakening, 1625–1760.* New York: Oxford Univ. Press, 1988.

White, Hayden. *Tropics of Discourse: Essays in Cultural Criticism.* Baltimore and London: Johns Hopkins Univ. Press, 1978.

Winslow, Ola E. *Jonathan Edwards, 1703–1758: A Biography.* New York: Macmillan, 1941.

Yarbrough, Stephen R., and John C. Adams. *Delightful Conviction: Jonathan Edwards and the Rhetoric of Conversion.* Westport, Conn.: Greenwood Press, 1993.

INDEX

The Self and the Sacred was typeset on a Macintosh computer system using PageMaker software. The text is set in Granjon and the chapter openings in Futura Book. This book was designed by Todd Duren, composed by Kimberly Scarbrough, and manufactured by Thomson-Shore, Inc. The recycled paper used in this book is designed for an effective life of at least three hundred years.